D0512807

Vocabulary for GCSE French

Philip Horsfall and David Crossland

MARY GLASGOW PUBLICATIONS

We are grateful to the following for allowing us to reproduce published material: La Nouvelle République du Centre-Ouest, Le Courrier de l'Ouest (p79). Every effort has been made to trace the copyright holders but the publishers will be pleased to make the necessary arrangements at the first opportunity if there are any omissions.

Designed by Ennismore Design, London

First published in 1997 by
Mary Glasgow Publications
an imprint of Stanley Thornes (Publishers) Ltd
Ellenborough House
Wellington Street
Cheltenham
GLOS GL50 1YW

98 99 00 01 02 / 10 9 8 7 6 5 4 3 2

A catalogue record for this book is available from the British Library.

ISBN 0 7487 2853-8

Printed and bound in Great Britain
by T. J. International Ltd., Padstow, Cornwall

Contents

Introduction

You will need a wide vocabulary both to understand and to make yourself understood in a variety of situations in the GCSE French exam. You can use this book throughout Years 10 and 11, to help you find useful words and phrases for each French topic area, and to give you hints about how to learn and prepare yourself for your exam.

This book sets out topic by topic the main vocabulary for **Foundation Tier**. It cannot include every word, as you may still meet some unknown words even at Foundation Tier (some of which you will not need to understand, others which you can look up in a dictionary). The words are grouped in short blocks of words that go together in some way, so that you will find them easier to learn.

Many of the words are presented in phrases which you could use in your speaking or writing exams, or when writing a letter. In the school section there is a full list of the French instructions you will find at the start of each question in the exam. Word games and puzzles are provided to help you practise the words as well.

The foundation words given in this book are taken from the five exam boards' lists. To make learning easier for you, some words and phrases are printed in blue. These are important words and phrases that everybody should learn thoroughly because, in our opinion and experience, they are the most useful and the most likely to appear in your exam. However, these words and phrases form a minimum, so if you are aiming for a top grade, you will need to learn many of the other words as well.

There are also some examples of words and phrases which might be useful for **Higher Tier**, based on the exam syllabuses, with spaces for you to write in your own extra words. Throughout the book you can customise our suggested phrases by writing in the boxes marked *Mes notes personnelles*.

At the end of each topic area you will find a section called **Seven steps to success**. This is a selection of tips on how to learn vocabulary, how to use a dictionary, and advice on listening, speaking, reading and writing activities plus specific exam tips. Together, these pages will help you to prepare for your GCSE French exam with confidence.

School

CLASSROOM OBJECTS

◆ **Foundation words**

le cahier	exercise book	la règle	ruler
le livre	book	la calculatrice	calculator
la page	page	le classeur	file
le bic	ballpoint pen	le cartable	school bag
le stylo	fountain pen	les ciseaux	scissors
le crayon	pencil	le tablier	apron
la trousse	pencil case	le tableau	board
la gomme	rubber	la fenêtre	window

WORKING IN THE CLASSROOM

◆ **Foundation words**

comprendre	to understand	s'excuser	to apologise
arrêter	to stop	fermer	to close
entrer	to go in	ouvrir	to open
sortir	to go out, take out	montrer	to show
demander	to ask	trouver	to find
corriger	to correct	perdre	to lose
se tromper	to make a mistake	prêter	to lend
avoir tort	to be wrong		
avoir raison	to be right	la chose	thing
oublier	to forget	un exemple	example
se souvenir (de)	to remember	le mot	word
se dépêcher	to hurry up	la phrase	sentence
deviner	to guess	la question	question
écrire	to write	une épreuve	test
parler	to speak	une erreur	mistake
écouter	to listen	la faute	error
		le titre	title
dire	to say	le silence	silence
dessiner	to draw	un accent	accent
lire	to read		
travailler	to work	un uniforme	uniform
essayer	to try	absent	absent
entendre	to hear	bravo	great, well done
répéter	to repeat	excellent	excellent
expliquer	to explain	compliqué	complicated
tricher	to cheat	encore une fois	once more
aider	to help	fort	loud(ly)

lentement	slowly	juste	correct
correct	correct	vrai	true
exact	correct	faux	false

What are these signs telling you to do?

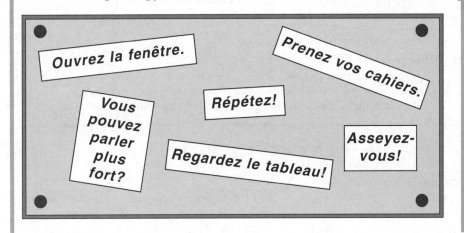

◆ Foundation phrases

Ne parlez pas anglais.	Don't speak English.
Ouvrez vos cahiers.	Open your exercise books.
Tu as oublié ton livre?	Have you forgotten your book?
Répétez en français.	Repeat in French.
Tu peux essuyer le tableau?	Can you wipe the board?
Ouvrez votre livre à la page vingt-trois.	Open your book at page 23.
Je ne comprends pas.	I don't understand.
Je ne sais pas.	I don't know.
Qu'est-ce que c'est en français/anglais?	What is it in French/English?
Que veut dire ce mot?	What does this word mean?
Tu peux me prêter ta règle?	Can you lend me your ruler?
Je ne trouve pas mon crayon.	I can't find my pencil.
J'ai perdu ma gomme.	I've lost my rubber.
Vous pouvez m'aider?	Can you help me?
Je peux aller aux toilettes?	Can I go to the toilet?
Voulez-vous répéter la question?	Will you repeat the question?
Pardon, pouvez-vous parler plus fort?	Sorry, could you speak louder?
Je me suis trompé.	I've made a mistake.
Tu as raison.	You're right.

◆ Higher words

You might also need these words:

prononcer	to pronounce	
discuter	to discuss	
une expression	expression	
le/la pensionnaire	boarder	
faire l'appel	to take the register	

Add any other useful words here:

....

....

....

◆ Higher phrases

Je m'entends bien avec mes profs.	I get on well with my teachers.
Comment est-ce que cela se prononce?	How do you pronounce that?
Il est interdit de fumer au collège.	You aren't allowed to smoke at school.

PLACES IN SCHOOL

◆ Foundation words

rentrer	to return		une école primaire	primary school
venir	to come		la cantine	canteen
commencer	to begin		la cour	playground
finir	to finish		le laboratoire	laboratory
terminer	to end		la salle	classroom
durer	to last		la salle des professeurs	staffroom
			le gymnase	gym
une école	school		la bibliothèque	library
le collège	secondary school			
le lycée	6th form college		premier	first
une école maternelle	nursery school		dernier	last

◆ Higher words

You might also need these words:

le vestiaire	changing room
le laboratoire de langues	language lab
un atelier	workshop
le casier	pigeon-hole, locker

Add any other useful words here:

....

....

....

◆ Higher phrases

Je n'aime pas travailler dans le laboratoire de langues.	I don't like working in the language lab.
C'est une école mixte.	It's a mixed school.

SUBJECTS

◆ Foundation words

la matière	subject	la langue	language
l'emploi du temps	timetable	le français	French
le cours	lesson	l'espagnol	Spanish
la leçon	lesson	l'allemand	German
l'enseignement	teaching, education	l'anglais	English
		l'éducation physique (EPS)	PE
les sciences	science	l'EMT	technology
la chimie	chemistry	la technologie	technology
la biologie	biology	les travaux manuels	handicrafts
la physique	physics	la géographie	geography
les maths	maths	l'histoire	history
l'informatique	information technology	la religion	RE
		le sport	sport
le dessin	art	la gymnastique	gymnastics
la musique	music	obligatoire	compulsory

◆ Foundation phrases

L'école commence à quelle heure?	When does school begin?
Le premier cours commence à neuf heures cinq.	The first lesson starts at five past nine.
L'après-midi, les cours finissent à quatre heures moins vingt.	In the afternoon, lessons end at three forty.
On a cinq cours par jour.	We have five lessons per day.
Les cours durent cinquante minutes.	Lessons last fifty minutes.
Le français est obligatoire.	French is compulsory.
J'apprends le français depuis cinq ans.	I've been learning French for five years.
Ma matière préférée, c'est l'espagnol.	My favourite subject is Spanish.

What subjects are on these stickers?

j'adore ♥ le français

– Vive le dessin! –

Le sport, c'est fantastique!

Les maths sont super!

```
┌─────────────────┐
│  MES NOTES      │
│  PERSONNELLES   │
│                 │──────────────────────────────────────────
│  Mon Ecole      │   L'école commence à
│                 │──────────────────────────────────────────
└─────────────────┘   Le premier cour commence à
                      ──────────────────────────────────────
                      Un cours dure
        ──────────────────────────────────────────────────
        On a          cours par jour.
        ──────────────────────────────────────────────────
        J'apprends                    depuis
        ──────────────────────────────────────────────────
        Ma matière préférée, c'est
        ──────────────────────────────────────────────────
```

◆ **School crossword**

a) Unscramble each school word below.

SURCO	cours	UNGEAL	....
RIOTISHE	....	CEELY	....
IMICHE	....	LONGPEAS	....
RUDER	....	ONCLE	....
LAVATRI	....	ECCINESS	....

b) Now fit the words into this grid.

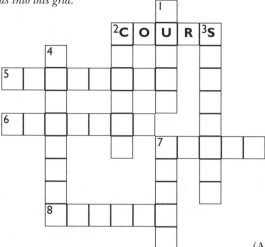

(Answer on page 111)

EXAMS AND TESTS

◆ **Foundation words**

examiner	to test, examine	traduire	to translate
un examen	exam	une exercice	activity, exercise
le travail	work	réussir	to succeed
une épreuve	test	échouer	to fail
le Bac	A-levels	la note	mark
étudier	to study	la qualification	qualification
apprendre	to learn	le bulletin	report
pratiquer	to practise	redoubler	to repeat the year

◆ **Foundation phrases**

Je n'aime pas les épreuves.	I don't like tests.
J'ai besoin d'une bonne note en maths.	I need a good grade in maths.
Je vais sûrement échouer en chimie.	I'll certainly fail in chemistry.
Je vais entrer en seconde.	I'm going into year 12.

MES NOTES PERSONNELLES

Mes Examens

J'ai besoin d'une bonne note en _____

_____

_____

Je vais sûrement réussir en _____

_____

◆ **Higher words**

You might also need these words:

la terminale	year 13
écrit	written
oral	oral
en majuscules	in block capitals
en minuscules	in small letters
entre parenthèses	in brackets
la moyenne	average mark
à refaire	to be done again

Add any other useful words here:

◆ **Higher phrases**

Je prépare un bac professionel.	I'm doing a GNVQ course.
Je suis en terminale.	I'm in year 13.

EXAM LANGUAGE

Change/Changez ... la carte postale	**Change** ... the postcard
Réponds/Répondez ... aux questions	**Answer** ... the questions
Décris/Décrivez ... les images	**Describe** ... the pictures
... ce que tu as/vous avez fait	... what you did
Complète/Complétez ... le tableau	**Complete** ... the table
... le plan	... the timetable
Explique/Expliquez ... ce qui s'est passé	**Explain** ... what has happened
Remplace/Remplacez ... les images avec des mots	**Replace** ... the pictures with words
Raconte/Racontez ... ce qui s'est passé	**Say** ... what happened
Remplis/Remplissez ... le tableau	**Fill in** ... the table
... les blancs	... the gaps
... les bulles	... the speech bubbles
Donne/Donnez ... des renseignements sur	**Give** ... information about
Coche/Cochez ... la bonne réponse	**Tick** ... the correct answer
Ecoute/Ecoutez ... la conversation	**Listen to** ... the conversation
Indique/Indiquez ... la bonne réponse	**Tick** ... the right answer
... A, B, C ou D	... A, B, C or D
... la bonne lettre	... the correct letter
Corrige/Corrigez ... les phrases suivantes	**Correct** ... the following sentences
Lis/Lisez ... l'article	**Read** ... the article
Dessine/Dessinez ... une flèche	**Draw** ... an arrow
Fais/Faites ... une liste	**Make** ... a list
Mets/Mettez ... dans le bon ordre	**Put** ... in the correct order
Ecris/Ecrivez ... une réponse à la lettre	**Write** ... an answer to the letter
... un rapport	... a report
... le bon numéro	... the right number
Regarde/Regardez ... les images	**Look at** ... the pictures
Pose/Posez des questions sur ...	**Ask** questions about ...
Imagine/Imaginez que ...	**Imagine** that ...
Cherche/Cherchez ... les bons numéros	**Look for** ... the right numbers
Souligne/Soulignez ...	**Underline** ...
Fais/Faites correspondre ... les phrases	**Join up** ... the parts of the sentence
Compare/Comparez ... ces phrases avec le texte	**Compare** ... these sentences with the text
Choisis/Choisissez ... la bonne phrase	**Choose** ... the correct sentence
... la bonne image	... the correct picture
Utilise/Utilisez ... ces symboles pour ...	**Use** ... these symbols to ...
Demande/Demandez ... les informations suivantes	**Ask for** ... the following information
Quel mot manque?	**Which** word is missing?

OUT OF LESSONS

◆ Foundation words

discuter	to discuss	le déjeuner	lunch
rencontrer	to meet	la pause déjeuner	midday break
bavarder	to chat	la récréation	play time, break
		un échange	exchange
le copain	friend (m)	le trimestre	term
la copine	friend (f)		

◆ Foundation phrases

Le déjeuner est à midi.	Lunch is at midday.
Je mange normalement à la cantine.	I normally eat in the canteen.
Je rencontre mes copains.	I meet my friends.
Nous jouons au ballon dans la cour.	We play ball in the playground.
On va en ville.	We go into town.

MES NOTES PERSONNELLES

Ma Pause Déjeuner

Le déjeuner est à _____

Pendant la pause déjeuner, je _____

avec _____

Quelquefois _____

_____

◆ Higher words

You might also need these words:

une excursion scolaire	school trip
un échange scolaire	school exchange
la réunion parents-professeurs	parents evening
la retenue	detention

Add any other useful words here:

....

....

....

....

◆ Higher phrases

Demain on fera une excursion scolaire.	Tomorrow we'll go on a school trip.
Nous avons un jour de congé.	We've got a day off.

DESCRIBING SCHOOL AND PEOPLE

◆ Foundation words

aimer	to like	faible	weak, not good at a subject
détester	to hate		
les devoirs	homework	fort	strong, good at a subject
affreux	awful	génial	great
difficile	difficult	intéressant	interesting
dur	hard	longtemps	long time
ennuyeux	boring	punir	to punish
facile	easy	sympa	nice

◆ Foundation phrases

Je fais deux ou trois heures de devoirs par soir.	I do two or three hours of homework every evening.
Je fais mes devoirs dans ma chambre.	I do my homework in my bedroom.
Mon père m'aide parfois.	My dad sometimes helps me.
Je suis fort(e) en anglais.	I'm good at English.
A mon avis, la musique est difficile.	In my opinion, music is hard.

MES NOTES PERSONNELLES

Mon Travail Scolaire

Je fais _____ de devoirs.

Je fais mes devoirs dans _____

Je suis fort(e) en _____

mais faible en _____

A mon avis, _____ est _____

◆ Higher words

You might also need these words:

fatigant	tiring
strict	strict
supplémentaire	extra

Add any other useful words here:

....

....

◆ Higher phrases

Notre prof de maths est gentil(le).	Our maths teacher is very nice.

PEOPLE IN SCHOOL

◆ **Foundation words**

le directeur	headmaster	un instituteur	primary school teacher (m)
la directrice	headmistress		
le professeur	teacher	une institutrice	primary school teacher (f)
un(e) élève	pupil		
un(e) étudiant(e)	student	le/la camarade de classe	classmate
le/la surveillant(e)	supervisor		

◆ **Foundation phrases**

Mon professeur de français s'appelle Mme. Smith. My French teacher is called Mrs Smith.

Il y a mille élèves dans mon collège. There are a thousand pupils in my school.

◆ **Higher words**

You might also need these words:

la femme de ménage	cleaning lady
le remplaçant	supply teacher
le concierge	caretaker
un(e) assistant(e)	foreign language assistant

Add any other useful words here:

....

....

....

....

....

◆ **Higher phrases**

On a un remplaçant pour les maths depuis longtemps. We've had a supply teacher for maths for a long time.

HIGHER EDUCATION

◆ **Foundation words**

améliorer	to improve	le dossier	project
le résultat	result	déçu	disappointed
une université	university	le diplôme	qualification
le progrès	progress	le niveau	level

S·EVEN STEPS TO SUCCESS

1 VOCABULARY

When you learn new words, set yourself some small tests to see how well you have learned them. One way is to make up anagrams by jumbling up the letters in a word or phrase. You then try to solve your own anagrams the next day.

To start you off, have a go at these anagrams:

teacher = FREEPORSUS (*professeur* in the wrong order)

1 *canteen* = LA NTIANEC ....

2 *lessons* = LES CORUS ....

3 *English is my favourite subject.* = L'LSGAAIN TES AM ÈIEMRTA ÉÉRÉEFRP

....

4 *Look at the board.* = GRDEAZRE EL EAULATB

....

(Answer on page 111)

2 DICTIONARY

At the end of the GCSE writing exam, your dictionary could help you to check the spelling of words.

Look at this short section of a letter, and use a dictionary to find and correct the three words spelled wrongly:

Ma matier préférée, c'est la geographe, mais je trouve le dessin très ennyeux.

(Answer on page 111)

3 LISTENING

When listening to people talking about something, try to think what you have been taught about that topic in your French lessons. For example, you will probably have been taught about French pupils not wearing uniform, having a longer school day than you and having no school on Wednesdays sometimes, so use that information to help you understand phrases like:

Il n'y a pas d'école le mercredi.

Nous n'avons pas d'uniforme scolaire.

4 SPEAKING

Always try to adapt the structures used in the sample phrases in this book to your own situation. For example, write out the phrase *L'école finit à cinq heures* as *L'école finit* .... then fill in the correct answer for your school. Try the same with these phrases:

Our set phrase	**Your version**
Ma matière préférée, c'est l'informatique.	....
Je viens au collège en autobus.	....
Un cours dure quarante-cinq minutes.	....
J'aime la musique, parce que c'est facile.	....

Throughout this book you can customise your own phrases in the boxes marked **Mes notes personnelles**.

5 READING

Some of what you have to read will be in real French handwriting: get used to the way the French write. Look at this French sentence containing all the letters of the alphabet, and underline those letters which are difficult for English readers.

Qu'est-ce que vous voyez à Londres, Geoffroi? Les beaux jardins de Kew, par exemple, hein?

6 WRITING

Look back over recent work that you have had marked. Are there little mistakes that you keep making? If so, make a list of them. In the exam, or when doing written coursework, check through your work when you have finished, looking for only these mistakes one at a time. Some typical examples are forgetting to make adjectives (describing words) agree with nouns, such as adding an extra "e" or "s", commonly misspelt words and important accents which change the meaning of a word.

7 EXAM WORK

On page 12 you saw the kind of instructions that will be on the exam paper. But if you forget what some of them mean, don't panic. Often there is an example which is done for you on the exam paper to show you what you have to do. Use the example to help you understand the instruction, or use your dictionary. Remember that you aren't allowed to ask your teacher in the exam!

The World of Work

FURTHER EDUCATION AND TRAINING

◆ Foundation words

travailler	to work	l'avenir (m)	future
rêver	to dream	les vacances	holidays
rester	to stay	bonne chance	good luck
taper	to type	riche	rich
penser	to think	pauvre	poor
		peut-être	perhaps
la carrière	career	plus tard	later
le boulot	work		
le travail	work	continuer	to continue
le métier	job	décider	to decide
la profession	profession	espérer	to hope
la compagnie	company	passer	to spend (time)
le salaire	salary	quitter	to leave

◆ Foundation phrases

Qu'est-ce que tu fais après les examens?	What are you doing after the exams?
Qu'est-ce que tu veux faire plus tard?	What do you want to do later?
Je voudrais aller à l'université.	I'd like to go to university.
Je vais quitter l'école.	I'm going to leave school.
Je voudrais bien commencer à travailler.	I'd quite like to start to work.
Après les examens, j'espère rester à l'école.	After the exams, I hope to stay at school.
L'année prochaine, j'espère préparer mon bac.	Next year, I hope to start my A-levels.
J'espère continuer mes études.	I hope to continue my studies.
Je vais faire anglais et français.	I'm going to do English and French.
Je veux être professeur.	I want to be a teacher.
Si j'ai de bons résultats, je continuerai mes études.	If I get good results, I'll stay on at school.

MES NOTES PERSONNELLES

Mon Avenir

Après les examens je voudrais _____

_____

Plus tard je veux _____

J'espère _____

◆ **Higher words**
You might also need these words:

le lycée technique	technical college
un apprentissage	apprenticeship
la variété	variety

Add any other useful words here:

....

....

....

◆ **Higher phrases**

Je voudrais travailler avec les gens.	I want to work with people.
Je n'ai pas de projets particuliers.	I don't have any definite plans.

L O O K I N G   F O R   A   J O B

◆ **Foundation words**

trouver	to find	le chômage	unemployment
poser sa candidature	to apply	le chômeur	unemployed person
chercher	to look for	un emploi	job
		la formation	training
le stage	course, work placement	expérimenté	experienced

◆ **Foundation phrases**

Mon frère est au chômage.	My brother is unemployed.
Il cherche du travail.	He's looking for work.
Il cherche depuis six mois.	He's been looking for six months.
Il n'a rien trouvé.	He's not found anything.
Ça doit être très difficile.	That must be very difficult.

◆ **Higher words**
You might also need these words:

le salarié	wage earner
attiré par	attracted by

Add any other useful words here:

....

....

◆ **Higher phrases**

Je suis attiré par une carrière dans l'armée.	I'm attracted by a career in the army.
On m'a conseillé de gagner un peu d'expérience pratique.	I've been advised to get some practical experience.

CAREERS AND EMPLOYMENT

◆ Foundation words

la profession	profession	le caissier	cashier
le patron	boss	la caissière	
la patronne		le/la secrétaire	secretary
un homme d'affaires	businessman	le/la dactylo	typist
la femme d'affaires	businesswoman	un(e) informaticien(ne)	computer operator
un agent de police	police officer		
le médecin	doctor		
le/la dentiste	dentist	le maçon	builder
un infirmier	nurse	un ouvrier	worker
une infirmière		une ouvrière	
un(e) avocat(e)	lawyer	le peintre	painter
le/la comptable	accountant	le chauffeur	driver
le gendarme	policeman	le facteur	postman
le/la vétérinaire	vet	le fermier	farmer
		la fermière	
le vendeur	salesman	un agriculteur	farmer
la vendeuse	saleswoman	le/la garagiste	garage worker
un épicier	grocer	le/la mécanicien(ne)	mechanic
une épicière		un(e) électricien(ne)	electrician
le boucher	butcher	le plombier	plumber
la bouchère			
le boulanger	baker	le garçon de café	waiter
la boulangère		le serveur	waiter
le/la marchand(e) de fruits	fruit seller	la serveuse	waitress
		une hôtesse de l'air	air hostess
le/la marchand(e) de légumes	greengrocer	le coiffeur	hairdresser
		la coiffeuse	
		la ménagère	housewife

◆ Foundation phrases

Mon père est agriculteur.	My dad is a farmer.
Ma cousine espère être coiffeuse.	My cousin hopes to be a hairdresser.
Qu'est-ce qu'elle fait dans la vie?	What job does she do?
Elle travaille comme chauffeur.	She works as a driver.
Quel est son métier?	What's her job?
Elle travaille dans une grande usine.	She works in a big factory.
J'ai travaillé dans un magasin pendant les vacances.	I worked in a shop during the holidays.
Je travaille le week-end dans un magasin en ville.	At the weekend, I work in a shop in town.
J'y travaille depuis deux ans.	I've been working there for two years.

◆ Higher words

You might also need these words:

le travail par roulement	shiftwork
une ambition	ambition
un emploi permanent	permanent job
le CV	CV

Add any other useful words here:

....

....

....

◆ Higher phrases

Je cherche un emploi qui m'offre de la sécurité.	I'm looking for a job with security.
Mon ambition est d'être pilote.	My ambition is to become a pilot.
Il travaille à son compte.	He's self-employed.

What jobs are being advertised?

■ OFFRES D'EMPLOIS

Recherche H., F., vendeur parfum cosmétique, maquillage grande qualité, % motivant, poss. promotion. Tél 02. 51.51.84.20

Embauche de suite maçons, région Niort. Tél. 05. 49.59.03.14 ou 05. 49.76.76.05.

Urgent, recherche serveuse restauration avec expérience. Tél. 49.05.50.54, ou Café de la Ville, place du Marché, Saint-Maixent-l'École

Restaurant le Victor cherche serveur(se), expérience exigée. Se présenter 685, route de Paris, Niort, Tél. 05. 49.44.26.54.

Cherche vendeuse bijouterie, expérience demandée. Envoyer C.V. + photo à Havas, N° 5091, B.P. 304, 79009 Niort Cedex.

What jobs are people looking for?

■ DEMANDES D'EMPLOIS

J.F. recherche emploi heures de ménage, garde enfants ou pers. âgées. Tél. 02. 43.67.23.98.

J.F. étudiante, BTS secrétaire, trilingue, 1re année, CHER. travail juillet, étudierait ttes prop. Tél. 02. 54.23.78.90.

Jeune homme recherche place chauffeur poids lourds, permis CL, C, expérience. Ecrire correspondant Nouvelle-République, 79330 Saint-Varent.

21

POCKET MONEY

◆ Foundation words

acheter	to buy	le cadeau	present
faire des économies	to save money	la livre sterling	pound sterling
gagner	to earn	le magasin	shop
distribuer	to deliver, give out	par mois	per month
faire du baby-sitting	to babysit	par semaine	per week
livrer	to deliver	les vêtements	clothes
payer	to pay	le journal (journaux)	newspaper(s)
		le week-end	weekend
l'argent de poche	pocket money	à mi-temps	part-time
la banque	bank	seulement	only

◆ Foundation phrases

J'ai cinq livres par semaine.	I have five pounds per week.
J'achète du maquillage.	I buy make-up.
Je fais des économies.	I save some money.
Je travaille pour mon beau-père pour gagner de l'argent.	I work for my step-father to earn some money.
Je ne travaille pas le week-end.	I don't work at the weekends.
Je distribue des journaux tous les matins.	I deliver newspapers every morning.
J'ai souvent fait du baby-sitting.	I've often done babysitting.
On me paie quatre livres par heure.	I get paid four pounds per hour.
Je trouve que c'est assez bien/mal payé.	I think it's fairly well/badly paid.

MES NOTES PERSONNELLES

Mon Argent

J'ai _____ par semaine.

J'achète _____

Pour gagner de l'argent je _____

◆ Higher words

You might also need these words:

		Add any other useful words here:
temporaire	temporary	
le pourboire	tip	....
satisfait	satisfied	
le compte bancaire	bank account	....

◆ Higher phrases

Je dépose mon argent sur mon compte.	I pay my money into my account.

SEVEN STEPS TO SUCCESS

1 VOCABULARY

To make learning French vocabulary more manageable, you need to decide which words are most important for you. Clearly if your father is a postman, then *le facteur* is a word you ought to know. You need to spend more time learning words like *bureau* and *chômage* that are more likely to appear in the texts you meet than *bouchère* or *avocat,* which you could always look up in a dictionary. Put these eight words to do with further education and work into the two categories. Compare your answers with those suggested on page 111.

Very useful for GCSE   **Less useful for GCSE**

....

....

....

....

....

expérimenté
le boulot
raccrochez
gagner
un médecin
l'avenir
un étudiant
un plombier

2 DICTIONARY

Many jobs in French have a masculine and a feminine form. The two most common ways of showing this are the *-euse* and the *-ière* endings on words for the feminine:

le vendeur (salesman)   *la vendeuse* (saleswoman)
le fermier (male farmer) ·   *la fermière* (female farmer)

Complete these sentences describing what some women do for a living:

1 Il est coiffeur et elle est ....

2 Il est épicier et elle est ....

3 Il est serveur et elle est ....

(Answer on page 111)

3 LISTENING

You will hear each item in your GCSE exam twice: therefore make notes in the margin while the tape is being played the first time and only fill in the full answer the second time. If you are taking the NEAB exam, you are allowed five minutes with a dictionary at the end, so use this time to check any of the answers you are unsure of.

4 SPEAKING
When talking about jobs in French, you rarely need a word for "the" or "a". You just say *Mon frère est pompier* for "My brother's a fireman" or *Ma cousine travaille comme secrétaire* for "My cousin works as a secretary".
Complete these sentences about your situation. Ask your teacher to check them:

Mon père/Ma mère est ....

Mon frère/Ma sœur travaille comme ....

Moi, je voudrais devenir ....

5 READING
Your answers will be marked according to whether you show that you have understood the passage, not according to how accurate your French grammar or spelling is. If you have to write an answer in French, you don't need to answer in a full sentence: often one word or a short phrase will do, providing you supply all the necessary information. For example, in answer to *Combien d'argent gagne-t-il par mois?* you need only to write the amount of money, *2000 francs*, rather than a full sentence such as *Il gagne deux mille francs par mois.*

6 WRITING
Use any time you have left at the end of a writing exam to check your grammar (one thing at a time: find and check all verbs, then all adjectives etc.). Check difficult spellings in the dictionary.
Here are three sentences written about a part-time job and future career with some grammatical errors and one typical spelling error in each. The mistakes have been underlined but not corrected. Can you complete the correction?

1 J'ai travaille tout les samedi dans un magasin en ville.
2 Ma sœur voudrais trouvé un emploi comme une hôtesse de l'air.
3 L'année dernier, pendant la vacance, j'ai cherché du travaille dans une usine.

(Answer on page 111)

7 EXAM WORK
Look carefully at how many marks each question is worth: if you are asked to give **two** details, make sure that you do. If a question is worth several marks, spend more time on it than a question worth one mark. If a question is worth four marks and you can only find three details, don't spend any longer on it, but come back to it in any time you have left at the end of the exam.

Public Services

POST

◆ Foundation words

la boîte aux lettres	letter box	envoyer	to send
la poste	post, post office	mettre à la poste	to post
le bureau de poste	post office	par avion	by air
le tabac	tobacconist's	pour	for
la lettre	letter	le timbre	stamp
la carte postale	postcard	se trouver	to be
le colis	parcel	un expéditeur	sender

◆ Foundation phrases

Où est la boîte aux lettres?	Where's the letter box?
Elle se trouve devant la poste.	It's in front of the post office.
Je voudrais envoyer une lettre en Angleterre.	I'd like to send a letter to England.
C'est combien pour envoyer une carte postale au Pays de Galles?	How much is it to send a postcard to Wales?
Je peux envoyer cette lettre par avion?	Can I send this letter by air?
Un timbre à deux francs cinquante, s'il vous plaît.	One two franc fifty stamp, please.
Donnez-moi deux timbres à trois francs.	Give me two three franc stamps.

◆ Higher words

You might also need these words:

Add any other useful words here:

le mandat postal	postal order
le télégramme	telegram
la télécarte	phonecard
la levée	collection (mail)

....

....

....

....

....

◆ Higher phrases

Je peux envoyer un télégramme d'ici?	Can I send a telegram from here?
La prochaine levée est à quelle heure?	What time is the next collection?

TELEPHONE

◆ Foundation words

le téléphone	phone	laisser	to leave
la cabine téléphonique	phone box	le message	message
le coup de téléphone	phone call	le numéro	number
allô	hello (phone)	le prénom	first name
à l'appareil	speaking	public	public
composer un numéro	to dial a number	rappeler	to call back
		sonner	to ring
décrocher (le combiné)	to lift the receiver	la tonalité	dialling tone
		zéro	zero, nought
un indicatif	code	un annuaire	phone directory

◆ Foundation phrases

C'est de la part de qui?	Who's speaking?
Quel est votre numéro de téléphone?	What's your phone number?
C'est le zéro un, dix, quatorze, trente, cinquante-deux.	It's 01. 10. 14. 30. 52.
Vous connaissez l'indicatif?	Do you know the code?
Madame Dupont à l'appareil.	Mrs Dupont speaking.
Allô, est-ce que je peux parler à Martin, s'il vous plaît.	Hello, can I speak to Martin, please?
Est-ce que Catherine est là?	Is Catherine there?
Je voudrais téléphoner à mes parents.	I'd like to ring my parents.
Voulez-vous laisser un message?	Would you like to leave a message?
Est-ce qu'il peut me rappeler?	Can he call me back?
Ne quittez pas!	Don't hang up!
Pouvez-vous répéter, s'il vous plaît?	Can you say that again, please?

◆ Higher words

You might also need these words:

le faux numéro	wrong number
raccrocher	to hang up
le PCV	reversed charge call
passer	to connect

Add any other useful words here:

....

....

◆ Higher phrases

Est-ce que je peux faire un PCV?	Can I reverse the charges?
Je me suis trompé de numéro.	I've got the wrong number.
Vous pourriez me passer Madame Roux?	Could you put me through to Mrs Roux?
Je peux vous téléphoner directement?	Do you have a direct line?

Which countries are listed on this leaflet?

☎ Les indicatifs internationaux

La Belgique	00 32	L'Italie	00 39
Le Portugal	00 351	L'Autriche	00 43
La France	00 33	La Suisse	00 41
La Grande-Bretagne	00 44	L'Espagne	00 34
L'Irlande	00 353	Les États-Unis	00 1

BANK

◆ Foundation words

la banque	bank	le franc	franc
le chèque	cheque	la livre sterling	pound sterling
le chéquier	cheque book	mille	thousand
la carte bancaire	banker's card	la monnaie	change
le bureau de change	exchange office	la pièce	coin
le centime	centime	le billet	note
le chèque de voyage	traveller's cheque		

◆ Foundation phrases

Je voudrais changer cinquante livres sterling. — I'd like to change £50.

Vous acceptez les chèques de voyage? — Do you accept traveller's cheques?

Il faut aller au bureau de change. — You have to go to the exchange office.

Avez-vous des pièces de cinq francs pour le téléphone? — Do you have any five-franc coins for the phone?

◆ Higher words

You might also need these words: *Add any other useful words here:*

le taux du change	exchange rate
le carnet de chèques	cheque book
les frais (f)	expenses, fee
le compte (en banque)	(bank) account
déposer	to deposit
toucher de l'argent	to withdraw

◆ Higher phrases

Quel est le taux du change? — What's the exchange rate?

Combien est-ce que je peux retirer? — How much can I take out?

ADVERTISING

◆ Foundation words

une annonce	advert	mieux	better
un animateur	host, compère (m)	la mode	fashion
une animatrice	host, compère (f)	penser	to think
un avis	opinion	la photo	photo
la couleur	colour	la publicité	advert
formidable	great	la petite annonce	small advert
une image	picture	une affiche	poster

◆ Foundation phrases

A mon avis, cette publicité est formidable.	In my opinion, this advert is great.
Je déteste cette image.	I hate this picture.
Je n'aime pas la photo non plus.	I don't like the photo either.
Nous préférons cette publicité.	We prefer this advert.

◆ Higher words

You might also need these words:

le succès	success
le spot télévisé	TV commercial
la vente	sale
le faire-part	(wedding)
(de mariage)	announcement

Add any other useful words here:

....

....

....

◆ Higher phrases

Je ne m'intéresse pas à la publicité.   I'm not interested in advertising.

◆ Slogans

Match the slogans to the articles.

1 Elles ont toutes les couleurs de la vie.
2 La meilleure façon de marcher.
3 Au départ pour l'Angleterre, 60 navettes par jour.
4 Nos clients gardent longtemps leur voiture. Il faut dire qu'elles sont faites pour garder longtemps leur propriétaire.

a) VOLVO 850 ÉDITION LIMITÉE
b) LE SHUTTLE
c) LES PAGES JAUNES
d) CHAUSSURES EN GORE-TEX

(Answer on page 111)

MEDIA

◆ Foundation words

le curseur	cursor	fermer	to switch off
la disquette	floppy disc	allumer	to switch on
le satellite	satellite	sous-titré	sub-titled
le disque compact	CD	en version française	in French
enregistrer	to record		
en différé	pre-recorded	la radio	radio
en direct	live	la télévision	television
le télé-journal	TV news	le dessin animé	cartoon
le journal télévisé	TV news	une émission	programme
le téléspectateur	viewer	les informations (fpl)	the news
charger (un programme)	to load (a programme)	les actualités (fpl)	the news
		le fait divers	news item
un écran	screen	le film	film
		le film d'amour	romance
un acteur	actor	le film d'aventures	adventure film
une actrice	actress	le film policier	detective film
la vedette	star	le film comique	comedy
chanter	to sing	le film d'épouvante	horror film
le chanteur	singer (m)	le film de science-fiction	sci-fi film
la chanteuse	singer (f)	le western	western
célèbre	famous	la pièce de théâtre	play
classique	classical	le magazine	magazine
regarder	to watch	le journal	newspaper
écouter	to listen	un article	article

◆ Foundation phrases

Qu'est-ce qu'il y a à la télévision, ce soir?	What's on television this evening?
Il y a un bon film policier.	There's a good detective film.
C'est en version française?	Is it in French?
C'est sous-titré.	It's sub-titled.
Il y a une émission de musique classique.	There's a classical music programme.
Elle commence à huit heures.	It starts at eight o'clock.
Je peux regarder la télévision?	May I watch television?
J'ai vu un bon film hier soir.	I saw a good film last night.

What's on television tonight?

16.50	Dessin animé	**18.20**	Actualités régionales
17.10	Flash d'informations	**18.30**	Dune, *film américain de*
17.15	Météo		*science-fiction*
17.20	Sports dimanche soir		

MEDIA OPINIONS

◆ Foundation words

une opinion	opinion	extraordinaire	extraordinary
casse-pieds	annoying, boring	extrêmement	extremely
mauvais	bad	formidable	great
moche	ugly, lousy	génial	terrific
nul	no good	passionnant	exciting
pénible	painful	rire	to laugh
		sensass	fantastic
amusant	funny	super	super
drôle	funny		
chouette	great	*See page 14 for describing school and people.*	

◆ Foundation phrases

La vedette était sensass!	The star was fantastic!
Il s'agit d'une famille anglaise.	It's about an English family.
Je ne lis pas le journal, parce que c'est ennuyeux.	I don't read the paper, because it's boring.
J'aime bien regarder la télé.	I really like watching television.
Les films d'aventures sont passionnants.	Action films are exciting.
Je suis d'accord avec toi.	I agree with you.
Le programme était génial, non?	The film was terrific, wasn't it?
J'ai préféré le film d'épouvante.	I preferred the horror film.
C'était nul, n'est-ce pas?	It was no good at all, was it?
Ce n'était pas mal.	It wasn't bad.
Je trouve les westerns moches.	I find cowboy films terrible.
A mon avis, les films policiers sont affreux.	In my opinion, detective films are awful.
C'est le meilleur programme à la télé.	It's the best programme on television.

MES NOTES PERSONNELLES

Mon Opinion

A mon avis, les _____ sont _____

_____

Mon programme préféré, c'est _____

parce que _____

_____

_____

SEVEN STEPS TO SUCCESS

1 VOCABULARY

When you have learned the words to do with a topic, copy them out with all the vowels missing. Then do something else for a while, and when you come back to the words, see if you can still fill in the vowels correctly.

What are these words?

1 une d — sq — — tt — = *a floppy disc* ....

2 un — cr — n = *a screen* ....

3 les — ct — — l — t — s = *news* ....

4 les — nf — rm — t — — ns = *the news* ....

(Answer on page 111)

2 DICTIONARY

It's important that you know how quickly you can find a word in a dictionary in the exam, since every minute is precious.

Time yourself with a watch while you look up the first ten words in the advertising section on page 28. This will give you an idea of how few words you will be able to look up in the exam without running out of time.

3 LISTENING

It's vital to read and understand each question on the exam paper before listening to the tape, so that you are not just listening but listening out for specific information. For example, if you are asked to give somebody's opinion on a film, then listen out for words like *formidable, génial, passionnant, mauvais*. If there's a name in the question (a person, a town or a street), then think in advance how it will be pronounced so that you are listening out for it. There is a list of question words on page 109, and typical instructions telling you what you have to do to answer the question on page 12.

4 SPEAKING

Many of the role play situations in the exam will ask you to imagine you are on the phone, whatever the topic areas being talking about. It's therefore important that you have mastered these key phrases:

Allô. (*Your name*) à l'appareil.   Comment ça va?

Est-ce que je peux parler à (*other person's name*)?

Est-ce qu'il (elle) peut me rappeler?   Merci beaucoup. Au revoir.

5 READING

Use your general knowledge to help you to understand what you read. For example, look at the list of international dialling codes on page 27. You can guess what most of the countries are because they look much the same as their English equivalents and you might know some of the codes already. Remember to use any visual clues as well to help, such as the symbol of the phone.

6 WRITING

Some topic areas where you will need to talk a lot will hardly ever be written about (classroom commands, at a post office, public transport). That is because in the real world you need to be able to ask for a stamp or make a phone call, but not to write such information. Spend more time practising how to say phrases from these topics, and don't bother with writing except as a means to help you remember the words and phrases.

7 EXAM WORK

If you are asked to tick three boxes on a grid, do not tick more than three, or the examiner will not give you credit. Equally, if you have to choose between true or false, don't tick both. If you want to change your mind about an answer, make it absolutely clear which one you want the examiner to mark. The examiner cannot give you the benefit of the doubt if your answer is unclear.

Yourself and Others

PERSONAL DETAILS

◆ Foundation words

aîné	elder	le nom	name
cadet	younger	le prénom	first name
le bébé	baby		
le gosse	kid	la Grande-Bretagne	Great Britain
un(e) adolescent(e)	teenager	britannique	British
		anglais	English
un an	year	écossais	Scottish
la naissance	birth	gallois	Welsh
naître	to be born	irlandais	Irish
né le ...	born on the ...	la retraite	retirement
un anniversaire	birthday		
la date	date	toujours	always
les vœux	wishes	unique	only
s'appeler	to be called	en général	in general

◆ Higher words

You might also need these words:

le domicile	home address
majeur	of age (18 +)
mineur	under 18

Add any other useful words here:

....

....

◆ Higher phrases

J'ai beaucoup déménagé. I've moved house a lot.

C'est mon nom de famille. It's my surname.

Pouvez-vous me l'épeler? Can you spell it for me?

Fill in your details on this form:

Prénom _____

Nom de famille _____

Anniversaire _____

Date de naissance _____

Nationalité _____

FAMILY AND FRIENDS

◆ Foundation words

(les membres de)	(members of)	le jumeau/la jumelle	twin
la famille	the family	le beau-père	step-father
les parents	parents, relations	la belle-mère	step-mother
un enfant	child	le beau-fils	step-son
maman	mum	la belle-fille	step-daughter
la mère	mother	le demi-frère	half-brother
papa	dad	la demi-sœur	half-sister
le père	father	le veuf	widower
la fille	daughter, girl	la veuve	widow
le fils	son		
le garçon	boy	un(e) ami(e)	friend
la femme	woman, wife	l'amitié (f)	friendship
la sœur	sister	le/la camarade	friend
le frère	brother	aimable	likeable
le mari	husband	embrasser	to kiss
un époux	husband	faire la bise	to kiss on the
une épouse	wife		cheek
le/la fiancé(e)	fiancé(e)	faire la connaissance	to get to know
		célibataire	single
la grand-mère	grandmother	épouser	to marry
le grand-parent	grandparent	félicitations	congratulations
le grand-père	grandfather	fêter	to celebrate
la nièce	niece	les noces	wedding
le neveu	nephew	se marier	to get married
le/la cousin(e)	cousin	marié	married
la tante	aunt	divorcé	divorced
un oncle	uncle	séparé	separated

◆ Foundation phrases

J'habite avec mon père et ma belle-mère.	I live with my father and step-mother.
J'ai deux frères mais je n'ai pas de sœurs.	I've got two brothers but no sisters.
Je suis enfant unique.	I'm an only child.

MES NOTES PERSONNELLES

Ma Famille

J'habite avec _____

J'ai _____

_____

APPEARANCE

◆ Foundation words

les cheveux	hair	la barbe	beard
la couleur	colour	les lunettes	spectacles
roux	red (hair)		
châtain	chestnut	gros	fat
blond	blond	joli	pretty
court	short	laid	ugly
long	long	maigre	slim
frisé	curly	mince	thin

◆ Foundation phrases

J'ai les yeux bleus.	I've got blue eyes.
Ma sœur a les cheveux courts et noirs.	My sister has short, black hair.
Mon copain est mince et blond.	My friend is slim and blond.
Je porte des lunettes.	I wear glasses.

MES NOTES PERSONNELLES

Mon Portrait

J'ai les yeux _____

J'ai _____

_____

_____

_____

◆ Higher words

You might also need these words:

pareil	same
ressembler à	to resemble
de taille moyenne	of medium height
chauve	bald
la moustache	moustache

Add any other useful words here:

....

....

....

◆ Higher phrases

Je ressemble à ma mère.	I look like my mother.

CHARACTER AND FEELINGS

◆ Foundation words

le caractère	character	méchant	dangerous, nasty
fier	proud	gai	happy
bête	stupid	intelligent	intelligent
charmant	charming	maladroit	clumsy
la confiance	confidence	paresseux	lazy
content	happy	poli	polite
dynamique	dynamic	sage	well behaved
égoïste	selfish	sérieux	serious
se fâcher	to get angry	sympa(thique)	nice
fou (folle)	mad	timide	shy
vilain	nasty	triste	sad

◆ Foundation phrases

Je suis normalement sympa mais un peu réservé.	I'm usually friendly but a little shy.
Mon frère a un bon sens de l'humour.	My brother's got a good sense of humour.
C'est une personne aimable.	He/She is a likeable person.

◆ Higher words

You might also need these words:

raisonnable	sensible
avare	mean
insupportable	unbearable
honnête	honest
impatient(e)	impatient
modeste	modest

Add any other useful words here:

....

....

....

....

....

....

....

◆ Higher phrases

Je m'entends bien avec mes parents.	I get on well with my parents.
Il se met très vite en colère.	He gets angry very quickly.
Je ne peux pas la supporter.	I can't stand her.
Il est d'humeur changeante.	He's moody.

Fill in this form from a dating agency.

-- ✂

Trouvez votre partenaire idéal!

Test-Partenaire ♥

1. Monsieur ☐ Madame ☐

Nom de famille: _____

Prénom: _____

L'adresse: _____

Le code postal: _____

4. Votre apparence

Votre taille (cm): _____

Les cheveux _____

Apparence:
☐ solide   ☐ négligé   ☐ à la mode
☐ élégant   ☐ ordinaire   ☐ sportif

2. Notes personnelles

célibataire ☐   divorcé ☐   séparé ☐

Nationalité: _____

Date de naissance: _____

Religion: _____

Lieu de naissance _____

5. À quoi vous intéressez-vous?

Intellectuel	Pratique	Sportif
☐ La musique	☐ Bricoler	☐ Le ski
☐ Le théâtre	☐ Peindre	☐ Le tennis
☐ Le ballet	☐ Les photos	☐ La natation
☐ L'opéra	☐ Collectionner	☐ La voile
☐ La comédie	☐ Tricoter	☐ La pêche
☐ Le cinéma	☐ La cuisine	☐ L'équitation
☐ La télévision	☐ La musique	☐ Le football
☐ La lecture	☐ Danser	☐ Le patinage
☐ Autres:	☐ Autres:	☐ Autres:

3. Vos caractéristiques

☐ amusant   ☐ ambitieux   ☐ vif
☐ gourmand   ☐ ouvert   ☐ intelligent
☐ romantique   ☐ patient   ☐ généreux
☐ gentil   ☐ poli   ☐ agréable
☐ timide   ☐ sage   ☐ paresseux

Autres choses: _____

Signature: _____

-- ✂

Homme, 23 ans, libre, ouvert, sympa, aimant la vie et les voyages, désire rencontrer jeune femme 18-25 ans pour découverte intérêts communs.

Femme, 19 ans, mignonne, cultivée et sportive, cherche homme 20-25 ans généreux, non fumeur pour une relation sérieuse et durable.

PETS AND ANIMALS

◆ Foundation words

un animal	animal	le cheval	horse
le chat	cat	la vache	cow
le chien	dog	le taureau	bull
le cochon d'Inde	guinea pig	le cochon	pig
le lapin	rabbit	le mouton	sheep
le poisson (rouge)	(gold)fish	le coq	cockerel
le perroquet	parrot	le poulet	chicken
un oiseau	bird		
la perruche	budgie	un insecte	insect
la tortue	tortoise	une abeille	bee
la souris	mouse	la guêpe	wasp
le hamster	hamster	la mouche	fly
		le moustique	mosquito

◆ Foundation phrases

J'ai un chien qui a neuf ans.	I've got a dog that's nine years old.
Je n'ai pas d'animaux.	I don't have any pets.
Ma copine a deux chats et des poissons rouges.	My friend's got two cats and some goldfish.
Je n'aime pas les chevaux.	I don't like horses.
J'avais autrefois une souris blanche.	I used to have a white mouse.
Elle est morte l'année dernière.	It died last year.

◆ Higher words

You might also need these words:

aboyer	to bark
miauler	to miaow
la cage	cage
une écurie	stable, barn

Add any other useful words here:

....

....

What do these signs mean?

NE DONNEZ PAS DE NOURRITURE AUX PIGEONS

Souris à donner
Contactez le:
04-78-09-54-32

Chiens interdits

SEVEN STEPS TO SUCCESS

1 **VOCABULARY**
Write down the names of a friend, neighbour, some relatives, your pet, etc. Then write the correct word after them without looking them up. For example:

Simon Fenton est mon voisin.

Mon oncle s'appelle Gary.

Winifred est ma grand-mère.

2 **DICTIONARY**
The plural of most French nouns is formed as in English by adding "s". However there are some exceptions. For example, nouns which end in -al have a plural ending of -aux: *un animal – des animaux.* Many nouns ending with -u have a plural -ux: *un neveu – des neveux.*
Practise with your dictionary so that you get the following plurals correct:

1 un cheval ....

2 un jumeau ....

3 un journal ....

4 un chou ....

(Answer on page 111)

3 **LISTENING**
Train yourself to listen out for messages that are implied: at higher level the direct answer may not be given but you have to work out from what is said what a speaker's character or attitude is. For example, if the speaker says *Je ne fais jamais de sport,* then he/she is likely to be lazy. If the speaker says *Je vois très rarement mes grand-parents,* the he/she is clearly not close to them. Strong attitudes are often accompanied by words like *toujours* (always) and *jamais* (never); less strongly held opinions have words like *quelquefois* (sometimes) and *assez* (fairly).

4 **SPEAKING**
Never answer a question just with *oui* or *non.* Keep going and add extra facts. If you are asked *Tu as un animal à la maison?* then give several details: type of animal, name, age, size, colour, etc: *Oui, j'ai un chien qui a juste un an. Il est noir et blanc, et il s'appelle Mortimer. Il est très gentil.*
Give your own answer to this question:

Tu as un frère ou une sœur?

TIPS ◆ TIPS ◆ TIPS ◆ TIPS ◆ TIPS

5 ### READING
Usually the answers you need to find in a reading text are in the same order as the questions, so you could underline the sections on the exam paper where the answers are to be found, and put the question numbers in the margin next to these sections. Never be afraid to underline or make any other marks on your exam paper that might help you.

6 ### WRITING
Try to make your sentences longer with *qui: J'ai un copain qui s'appelle Jason.*
Nous avons un hamster qui a un an et un lapin qui habite dans le jardin.
Continue these sentences, and ask your teacher to check them:

J'ai un frère qui ....

Voici une photo de ma mère qui ....

J'avais autrefois un chien qui ....

7 ### EXAM WORK
Don't be put off by longer passages. Even very difficult passages can have quite easy questions on them, so never give up. The same applies to the exam as a whole: there are often easy questions scattered throughout the paper, so never give up, just miss out what you can't do for the moment and then go on to the next question.

Which sign of the zodiac are you?

Verseau   Taureau   Lion   Scorpion

Poisson   Gémeaux   Vierge   Sagittaire

Bélier   Cancer   Balance   Capricorne

Home Life

WHERE YOU LIVE

◆ **Foundation words**

habiter	to live	le pays	country
déménager	to move house	le quartier	part of town
une adresse	address	la rue	road, street
un appartement	flat	la route	road
une avenue	avenue	une H.L.M	council flat
le centre	centre	le studio	small flat, bedsit
le code postal	postcode	la banlieue	suburb
un endroit	place	le garage	garage
un étage	floor	un immeuble	block of flats
la maison	house	le bâtiment	building

◆ **Foundation phrases**

J'habite un petit appartement.	I live in a small flat.
Nous habitons dans le centre.	We live in the centre.
Mes grands-parents habitent un appartement, au quatrième étage.	My grandparents live in a flat, on the fourth floor.

◆ **Higher words**

You might also need these words:

louer	to rent
construire	to build
demeurer	to stay
aménager	to fit out, equip
le loyer	rent

Add any other useful words here:

....

....

◆ **Higher phrases**

La maison est en mauvais état.	The house is in poor condition.

What is being offered in these adverts?

A VENDRE
Pavillon jumelé
St-Benoît Chantejean

140 m², 5 ch. 2 s. de b.,
séjour, cheminée, terrasse,
terrain boisé, proximité
lycée, bus.
Tél. 02.87.09.45.32.

Sud Parthenay
maison, 5–6 pièces, entièrement rénovée,
jardin et dépendances, loyer 4 000 F/mois.
☎ **05.49.43.77.82.**

7 km environ de Parthenay
maison gatinaise 3 pièces avec poutres et
cheminée, salle d'eau, grenier aménageable
au-dessus, garage, terrain de 500m² environ

FURTHER DETAILS

◆ Foundation words

calme	quiet	le village	village
agréable	pleasant	la ville	town
ancien	old	la campagne	countryside
vieux	old	le bois	wood
neuf	brand new	la place	square
nouveau	new	le centre-ville	town centre
typique	typical		
beau	good looking	la vue	view
cher	expensive	électrique	electric
joli	pretty	dehors	outside
moderne	modern	un escalier	stairs
confortable	comfortable	en haut	upstairs
entouré de	surrounded by	en bas	downstairs
pratique	convenient		
étroit	narrow	la fleur	flower
loin de	far from	le bassin	pond
près de	near to	un arbre	tree
en face de	opposite	l'herbe (f)	grass
à côté de	next to	la pelouse	lawn
		le jardin (potager)	(vegetable) garden
le nord	the north		
l'est	the east		
l'ouest	the west		
le sud	the south		

◆ Foundation phrases

J'habite à ...	I live in ...
C'est dans le nord de l'Angleterre.	It's in the north of England.
Ma maison est assez grande.	My house is quite big.
Elle a trois chambres.	It's got three bedrooms.
Chez moi, nous avons un garage et un jardin.	We have a garage and a garden at home.
On est près du centre-ville.	We're near the town centre.
C'est un quartier agréable et calme.	It's a pleasant and quiet part of town.
Notre maison a deux étages.	Our house has got two floors.
C'est en brique rouge.	It's made of red brick.
Il y a des arbres derrière la maison.	There are some trees at the back of the house.

MES NOTES
PERSONNELLES

Ma Maison

J'habite à _____

C'est situé _____

_____

Chez moi, nous avons _____

_____

_____

◆ **Higher words**

You might also need these words:

tondre — to mow
un arbre fruitier — fruit tree
le pommier — apple tree
le papier peint — wallpaper
le volet — shutter

Add any other useful words here:

....

....

◆ **Higher phrases**

Ils veulent agrandir la maison. — They want to extend the house.
Nous avons aménagé la cuisine. — We've fitted out the kitchen.

◆ **Missing letters**

*Fill in the missing letters, then rearrange the seven
missing letters to make a piece of furniture.*

ROBIN — T

LA — PE

PL — FOND

TAP — S

PO — TE

F — UR

MU —

— — — — — — —

(Answer on page 111)

43

AROUND THE HOME

◆ Foundation words

la pièce	room	en bois	made of wood
la cuisine	kitchen	en métal	made of metal
la cave	cellar	en plastique	made of plastic
la chambre	bedroom		
une entrée	entrance	la moquette	fitted carpet
le vestibule	hall	un oreiller	pillow
la salle à manger	dining room	partager	to share
la salle de bains	bathroom	la photo	photo
la salle de séjour	living room	le poster	poster
le salon	lounge	le rez-de-chaussée	ground floor
les toilettes	toilet	le rideau	curtain
les WC	toilet	le tapis	carpet
le balcon	balcony	le chauffage central	central heating
le toit	roof	la cheminée	chimney,
le plafond	ceiling		fireplace
le plancher	floor		
le mur	wall		

◆ Foundation phrases

Chez moi, au rez-de-chaussée, il y a la salle à manger, la cuisine et le salon.	In my home, on the ground floor, there's the dining room, the kitchen and the lounge.
Dans ma chambre, on trouve mon lit, une armoire et un placard.	In my bedroom, there is my bed, a wardrobe and a cupboard.
Les murs sont blancs et rouges.	The walls are white and red.
Les rideaux sont bleus.	The curtains are blue.
J'ai ma propre chambre au premier étage.	I've got my own room on the first floor.

MES NOTES PERSONNELLES

Chez Moi

Chez moi, il y a

Dans ma chambre, on trouve

Les murs sont

Les rideaux sont

◆ **Higher words**

You might also need these words:

		Add any other useful words here:
le jardin d'hiver	conservatory	
le grenier	attic	....
le palier	landing	
le débarras	junk room	....

FURNITURE

◆ **Foundation words**

les meubles	furniture	le four (à micro-ondes)	(microwave) oven
une armoire	wardrobe		
une étagère	shelf	le frigo	fridge
la lampe	lamp	la machine à laver	washing machine
le lit	bed	le placard	cupboard
le réveil	alarm clock		
		le buffet	sideboard
le miroir	mirror	le canapé	settee
la glace	mirror	la chaîne-stéréo	stereo system
le bidet	bidet	la chaise	chair
la baignoire	bath tub	le fauteuil	armchair
le robinet	tap	le magnétophone	tape recorder
la douche	shower	le magnétoscope	video recorder
le lavabo	washbasin	le piano	piano
		la radio	radio
le lave-vaisselle	dishwasher	le téléphone	telephone
le congélateur	freezer	le répondeur téléphonique	answer-phone
la cuisinière (à gaz)	(gas) cooker	la table	table
un évier	sink	la télévision	television

◆ **Foundation phrases**

Dans le salon, il y a deux fauteuils.	There are two armchairs in the lounge.
Nous n'avons pas de douche.	We don't have a shower.

◆ **Higher words**

You might also need these words:

		Add any other useful words here:
un appareil	appliance	
une essoreuse	spin drier	....
la table de chevet	bedside table	
meublé	furnished	....

DAILY ROUTINE

◆ Foundation words

prendre	to take	le sommeil	sleep
s'habiller	to get dressed	le bain	bath
se déshabiller	to get undressed	l'eau (f)	water
se réveiller	to wake up	le gant de toilette	face cloth
s'endormir	to go to sleep	la serviette	towel
se raser	to shave	du shampooing	shampoo
se laver	to have a wash	du maquillage	make-up
se brosser les dents	to clean your teeth	la brosse à dents	toothbrush
se maquiller	to put on make-up	le dentifrice	toothpaste
		le savon	soap
froid	cold	le rasoir	razor
chaud	hot	le peigne	comb

◆ Foundation phrases

Je peux prendre un bain, s'il vous plaît?	Please may I have a bath?
J'ai pris une douche ce matin.	I had a shower this morning.
Il y a du shampooing dans le placard.	There's shampoo in the cupboard.
Votre serviette est dans la salle de bains.	Your towel is in the bathroom.
Tu as besoin de quelque chose?	Do you need anything?
J'ai oublié ma serviette.	I've forgotten my towel.
Je n'ai plus de dentifrice.	I've got no toothpaste left.

◆ Higher words

You might also need these words:

s'occuper de	to be busy with
faire la sieste	to have a nap
faire la toilette	to get washed
avoir l'occasion de	to have a chance to

Add any other useful words here:

....

....

....

....

....

◆ Higher phrases

Après m'être changé(e), je promène mon chien.	After getting changed, I walk the dog.
Mon grand-père faisait la sieste tous les jours.	My grandad used to have a nap every afternoon.

JOBS AROUND THE HOME

◆ Foundation words

acheter	to buy	faire le repassage	to do the ironing
aider	to help	repasser	to iron
passer l'aspirateur	to vacuum	faire le lit	to make the bed
balayer	to sweep	arroser	to water
faire les courses	to do the shopping	bricoler	to do odd jobs
faire le ménage	to do the housework		
faire la vaisselle	to do the washing up	les affaires	things
laver	to wash	un aspirateur	vacuum cleaner
mettre la table	to set the table	la cuisine	cooking
débarrasser	to clear	la lessive	washing
nettoyer	to clean	le jardinage	gardening
nourrir	to feed	la poubelle	dustbin
ranger	to tidy	le linge	linen, washing
travailler	to work	la nappe	tablecloth

◆ Foundation phrases

Je fais les courses.	I do the shopping.
Hier, j'ai fait la lessive.	Yesterday I did the washing.
Généralement, ma mère fait la cuisine.	Generally, my mother does the cooking.
Mon père fait la vaisselle.	My dad washes up.
Je sors la poubelle.	I put the dustbin out.
Mon père cultive des légumes.	My dad grows vegetables.

◆ Higher words

You might also need these words: *Add any other useful words here:*

éplucher	to peel
essuyer	to wipe
rénover	to renovate
enlever la poussière	to dust

....

....

MES NOTES PERSONNELLES

J'aide à la Maison

Pour aider à la maison, je _____

_____

Généralement, mon père/ma mère _____

_____

SEVEN STEPS TO SUCCESS

1 **VOCABULARY**
The accent is part of the spelling of some French words as it often changes the pronunciation just as much as any letter. As you learn key phrases from each section, write them out without the accents, then see if you can fill them in correctly a day or so later. Put the missing accents on these three sentences:

1 Generalement mon pere fait le menage apres le diner.

2 La chaine-stereo est a cote de la television.

3 Nous avons demenage l'annee derniere.

(Answer on page 111)

2 **DICTIONARY**
One way of improving your dictionary use is to speed up your mastery of alphabetical order.
Write the words from this box in the correct alphabetical order as quickly as possible (if you can work with a partner, try this as a race). Remember that accents on letters do not affect the alphabetical order.

> campagne, chaise, calme, cheminée, chaîne-stéréo, cher, cave, chauffage, canapé, cuisine, congélateur, chambre

(Answer on page 111)

3 **LISTENING**
Quite a lot of what you hear will not be necessary to answer the questions, so don't worry if there are bits you don't understand. Look carefully at the question set: is it asking for a certain detail or for an overall impression? Then try to pick out the words and phrases to do with that. For example, if you know that you have to say at what time somebody gets up, listen out for *lever* and a time after the word *à/vers*. You may actually hear *Mon réveil sonne à sept heures et demie, mais, je ne me lève qu'à huit heures moins vingt*. In this case, the first half of the sentence is not relevant to the question being asked.

4 **SPEAKING**
Listen to your teacher's questions for the clues to what you must say in the oral exam: if you are asked *Quelles pièces y a-t-il chez toi?* then you need to name more than one room. If you are asked *Qu'est-ce que tu as fait ce matin avant de venir au collège?* then you need to answer using a past tense.

5 READING

Although some words in French look the same as, or very similar to, English words, their meanings are not always identical. However, they may give you a clue about the meaning, and this will help you remember them. For example, *une cave* is a dark and gloomy place, like a cellar; *une serviette* is a piece of cloth, like a towel.

Work out your own way of remembering the following meanings:

un studio = a small flat

un escalier = stairs

une pièce = a room

un buffet = a sideboard

6 WRITING

You often need to ask questions in a letter, so make sure you know how to do so with phrases like *A quelle heure ...? Combien de ...? Est-ce qu'il y a ...? Tu as ...?*
What were the questions that received these replies?

1 Tu vas dormir dans le grenier. ....

2 Nous avons trois chambres. ....

3 Il n'y a pas de jardin chez nous. ....

4 Je n'ai pas d'animaux. ....

(Answer on page 111)

7 EXAM WORK

For reading and writing, it's probably best to tackle all the easy questions or sections first, and do not get stuck on any questions. When you have finished those you can do easily, go back and tackle the ones you missed out, using the dictionary to help. You can control the speed and the order in which you tackle the reading and writing papers. But don't forget to make a mental note to go back to the ones you've left!

Electro-Ménager

Vends Machine à laver Indésit état marché, 600 F. Tél. 02.32.65.81.76.

Vends Congélateur 510L, servi 3 ans, état neuf. Tél. 04.76.32.43.12.

Vends Canapé convertible + 2 fauteuils, bon état, petit prix. Tél. 02.54.32.65.32.

Vends Aspirateur 800 watts, bon état, cause double emploi. Tél. 05.45.76.21.22.

Vends Lit + literie + chevet, chambre enfants en pin naturel, état neuf, petit prix. Tél. 02.32.34.56.43.

Vends Frigo Philips, blanc, 270 L. avec congél. Tél. 05.56.67.54.34.

Health and Welfare

PARTS OF THE BODY

◆ Foundation words

le corps	body	le bras	arm
le sang	blood	la main	hand
la tête	head	le poing	fist
la figure	face	le doigt	finger
l'oeil (les yeux)	eye (eyes)	le cœur	heart
aveugle	blind	l'estomac	stomach
le nez	nose	le ventre	stomach
la lèvre	lip	le dos	back
la voix	voice	la jambe	leg
l'oreille	ear	le genou	knee
sourd	deaf	le talon	heel
la dent	tooth	le pied	foot
la joue	cheek		
le cou	neck	*See page 35 for describing people.*	
la gorge	throat		

◆ Foundation phrases

Il a un gros nez.	He's got a large nose.
De la tête aux pieds	From head to foot.
Donner un coup de pied à	To kick.

◆ Higher words

You might also need these words:

le doigt de pied	toe
la cheville	ankle
le front	forehead
handicapé physique	physically handicapped

Add any other useful words here:

....

....

....

....

....

....

◆ Higher phrases

Il s'est cassé la jambe.	He's broken his leg.
Je me suis foulé la cheville.	I've sprained my ankle.

I L L N E S S

◆ Foundation words

avoir mal à	to have a pain in	comme ci, comme ça	not bad
bouger	to move	chaud	hot
être enrhumé	to have a cold	fatigué	tired
se coucher	to go to bed	froid	cold
tousser	to cough	malade	ill
tomber malade	to fall ill	pas mal	not bad
dormir	to sleep	la douleur	pain
se sentir	to feel	une angine	sore throat
lever	to raise	le rhume	cold
avaler	to swallow	pâle	pale
souffrir	to suffer		

◆ Foundation phrases

Ça va bien/mal/mieux.	I'm fine/not well/better.
Je me sens malade.	I feel ill.
J'ai froid/chaud.	I'm cold/hot.
J'ai mal à la tête.	I've got a headache.
J'ai mal au dos.	My back hurts.
Je n'ai pas faim.	I'm not hungry.
Je peux me coucher?	Can I go to bed?
Je suis enrhumé.	I've got a cold.
Je me suis fait mal au genou.	I've hurt my knee.

Read these medicine labels.

posologie :
• 2 cuillerées à café (soit 10ml) 3 fois par jour après les 3 principaux repas et éventuellement, le soir au coucher

POSOLOGIE ET MODE D'EMPLOI
ADULTES (à partir de 15 ans) :
1 à 2 comprimés par prise, **1 à 3 fois** par 24 heures à 4 heures d'intervalle au minimum.
Avaler les comprimés avec une gorgée de liquide.

◆ Higher words

You might also need these words:

		Add any other useful words here:
la rougeole	measles	
suer	to sweat	....
vomir	to vomit	
trembler	to shiver	....

◆ Higher phrases

J'ai vomi deux fois.	I've been sick twice.
Ça fait mal depuis trois jours.	It has been hurting for three days.

RECOVERY AND EMERGENCY

◆ Foundation words

un accident	accident	la piqûre	injection, sting
une ambulance	ambulance	le sirop	cough mixture
urgent	urgent	du sparadrap	plaster
au secours!	help!	le comprimé	tablet
écraser	to run over	la drogue	drug
renverser	to knock over		
tomber	to fall	le chirurgien	surgeon
se faire mal	to hurt oneself	un opticien	optician
se noyer	to drown	guérir	to cure
		s'inquiéter	to be worried
antiseptique	antiseptic	sain	healthy
la crème (solaire)	(sun)cream	une insolation	sun stroke
la pastille	throat sweet	la maladie	illness
piquer	to sting	le fumeur	smoker

What do these signs mean?

DEFENSE de FUMER

ENTREE
Strictement RESERVEE
AUX AMBULANCES
ET AU CORPS MEDICAL

DANGER DE MORT
Accessible seulement au
personnel autorisé

SORTIE DE SECOURS

◆ Foundation phrases

Je suis tombé.	I fell down.
Ça fait mal quand je bouge.	It hurts when I move.
Je vais vous faire une piqûre.	I'm going to give you an injection.

◆ **Higher words**

You might also need these words: *Add any other useful words here:*

se remettre	to recover
le plâtre	plaster
la radiographie	x-ray

....

....

....

◆ **Higher phrases**

Remets-toi vite!	Get well soon!
Je voudrais me reposer un peu.	I'd like to lie down for a while.
Je dois faire un régime.	I must go on a diet.

SEVEN STEPS TO SUCCESS

1 VOCABULARY

Some words in English might help you remember parts of the body in French.
For instance "corpse" might help you remember *le corps*.
Which French words (parts of the body) do these English words make
you think of?

1 dental   ....

2 manual   ....

3 pedestrian   ....

(Answer on page 111)

2 DICTIONARY

As in all languages, some words in French have more than one meaning.
In your dictionary look up these words from this section to find meanings other
than the ones given:

1 la joue   ....

2 la douleur   ....

3 mal   ....

4 écraser   ....

5 la gorge   ....

(Answer on page 111)

T
I
P
S
◆
T
I
P
S
◆
T
I
P
S
◆

3 LISTENING

Listen out for French words that are very similar to English ones, but which are pronounced differently. Even quite puzzling sounds are sometimes easy when you see them written. For example: *allergie, estomac, corps, alcool, pastille.*

4 SPEAKING

In the exam preparation room, say things out loud to yourself if possible: it's easier to say a phrase like *Je voudrais quelque chose contre un coup de soleil* to your teacher once you have wrapped your tongue round it a few times in advance. Try saying these phrases out loud to yourself three times to help you to get to know them and to help you pronounce them better:

1 Je suis tombé de mon vélo et je me suis fait mal.

2 Ça va mieux, je n'ai plus mal aux oreilles.

3 Il me faut du sparadrap et de la crème antiseptique.

5 READING

If you have studied another language like Spanish or German, there may be words there that you have learned that will help you with French. For example, if you know that the German word *die Grippe* means the flu, then *la grippe* in French probably means the same. *Der Körper* in German might also help you with the meaning of *le corps.*

6 WRITING

Letters usually use paragraphs to break up text into separate ideas to make it easier to read. If the exam paper has a letter in four paragraphs, try to follow the same lay-out in your reply: it will make your answer look much better and it will be easier to read for the examiner.

7 EXAM WORK

When marking the written paper at higher tier, examiners are looking not just for you to get the message across, but also at the quality of your French. This includes such things as:

- getting the right form of the verb: *j'ai chaud* but *elle a chaud*
- some use of tenses other than the present: *j'ai souffert*
- some use of modals (*vouloir, pouvoir, devoir*): *mon copain devait rester à la maison*
- longer sentences: *ma sœur ne pouvait pas bouger, parce qu'elle avait mal au dos.*

Free Time

HOBBIES AND SPORT

◆ **Foundation words**

le sport	sport	se détendre	to relax
le football	football	gagner	to win
le tennis	tennis	jouer	to play
le hockey	hockey	le joueur	player
le ping-pong	table tennis	participer (à)	to take part (in)
la boxe	boxing	faire partie de	to belong to
la natation	swimming	collectionner	to collect
l'équitation (f)	horse riding		
le golf	golf	actif	active
faire des promenades	to go walking	le loisir	leisure
la randonnée	hike	le passe-temps	pastime
l'alpinisme (m)	climbing	la distraction	leisure activity
l'athlétisme (m)	athletics	une équipe	team
le basket	basketball	le match	match
les boules	bowls	le concours	competition
le cyclisme	cycling	le championnat	championship
le handball	handball	le jeu	game
le rugby	rugby	le match nul	draw
le ski	ski	un arbitre	referee
le ski nautique	water-skiing	le membre	member
les sports d'hiver	winter sports		
le volley	volleyball	lire	to read
la voile	sailing	la lecture	reading
		le roman	novel
le ballon	ball	la bande dessinée	comic
les cartes	cards	le dessin animé	cartoon
faire de la planche	to skateboard	un illustré	magazine
à roulettes		un écrivain	writer
les patins à roulettes	rollerskates		
plonger	to dive	un ordinateur	computer
attraper	to catch	les jeux vidéo	computer games
aller à la pêche	to go fishing	la chaîne	channel
la canne (à pêche)	fishing rod		
		coudre	to sew
le centre de loisirs	leisure centre	tricoter	to knit
la patinoire	skating rink	la photo	photo
la piste	track, ski run	prendre des photos	to take photos
le stade	stadium	la pellicule	film
le terrain	pitch, course	la pile	battery
la piscine	swimming pool	la peinture	painting

H/wk.

◆ Foundation phrases

Je joue au golf tous les samedis.	I play golf every Saturday.
J'aime faire de la planche à roulettes.	I like skateboarding.
Mon sport préféré, c'est le tennis.	My favourite sport is tennis.
Je suis membre d'une équipe de football.	I'm a member of a soccer team.
Mes parents m'ont acheté un vélo tout terrain.	My parents bought me a mountain bike.
A la maison, je lis beaucoup de bandes dessinées.	I read a lot of comics at home.
Je joue aux cartes quelquefois.	I sometimes play cards.

MES NOTES PERSONNELLES

Mes Passe-temps

Mon sport préféré, c'est _____

Quelquefois, je joue _____

avec _____

A la maison _____

_____

_____

_____

_____

◆ Higher words

You might also need these words:

la musculation	body-building
l'aérobic	aerobics
une exposition	exhibition
s'entraîner	to train

Add any other useful words here:

....

....

....

....

◆ Higher phrases

J'étais autrefois un scout.	I used to be a scout.
Je m'entraîne trois fois par semaine.	I train three times a week.
J'adore faire de l'aérobic.	I like doing aerobics.

MUSIC AND FILMS

◆ Foundation words

la chanson	song	la séance	performance
le tube	hit song	le spectacle	show
la boîte de nuit	night club	le cinéma	cinema
danser	to dance	la salle (de cinéma)	cinema, screen
le bal	dance	un enfant	child
le concert	concert	un adulte	adult
		une entrée	ticket
la musique (pop)	(pop) music	un étudiant	student
un orchestre	orchestra	la place	seat
un instrument	instrument	le prix	price
la flûte à bec	recorder	le film	film
la guitare	guitar	le groupe	group
la trompette	trumpet	interdit	forbidden
le violon	violin	une ouvreuse	usherette
le piano	piano		

See page 26 for more about the media.

commencer — to begin
coûter — to cost

◆ Foundation phrases

Moi, j'aime beaucoup jouer de la guitare.	I very much like playing the guitar.
Je joue du violon depuis longtemps.	I've been playing the violin for a long time.
La séance commence à quelle heure?	When does the performance begin?
Le film finit à minuit.	The film finishes at midnight.
Il y a des réductions pour les étudiants?	Are there reductions for students?
Qu'est-ce qu'on joue ce soir?	What's on this evening?
C'est quelle sorte de film?	What sort of film is it?
Tu veux venir à ma fête samedi?	Do you want to come to my party on Saturday?
On va faire une promenade?	Shall we go for a walk?
Tu es libre, ce soir?	Are you free this evening?
Si on allait au café?	How about going to the café?
J'aimerais mieux aller à une discothèque.	I'd prefer to go to a disco.
Deux places pour la salle trois.	Two seats in screen three.
Ce film est interdit aux moins de dix-huit ans.	That film has an 18-certificate.

◆ Higher words

You might also need these words:

la fanfare	brass band
le soliste	soloist
la contrebasse	double bass
la batterie	drumkit

Add any other useful words here:

....

....

....

....

....

....

◆ Higher phrases

Je fais partie d'une fanfare. I'm a member of a brass band.
Jouer du piano, ça me fait plaisir. Piano-playing is fun.

◆ Film titles

a) What are these films called in English?

1 Le Roi Lion
2 La Guerre des Etoiles
3 Le Père de la Mariée
4 Les Dents de la Mer
5 Pour une Poignée de Dollars

b) Match the films with these descriptions:

a) un film de science-fiction
b) un western
c) un film d'aventures
d) un dessin animé
e) un film comique

(Answer on page 111)

TRIPS AND MEETINGS

◆ Foundation words

dépenser	to spend (money)	le bureau de renseignements	information office
visiter	to visit (place)	une excursion	trip
rendre visite à	to visit (person)	le cirque	circus
acheter	to buy	la foire	fair
attendre	to wait	la maison des jeunes	youth club
avoir lieu	to take place		
demander	to ask	le billet	ticket
inviter	to invite	la brochure	brochure
payer	to pay	le café	café
réserver	to reserve, book	le restaurant	restaurant
		le magasin	shop
proposer	to suggest	le musée	museum
réduit	reduced	le parc	park
jusqu'à	until	la personne	person
libre	free	la réduction	reduction
chez moi	at my house	le dépliant	leaflet
gratuit	free		
inclus	included	sortir	to go out
à partir de	from	le théâtre	theatre
sauf	except for	voir	to see
le syndicat d'initiative	tourist office		

See page 71 for more about socialising.

◆ Hobbies

Write the French hobby for these 6 pictures in order of preference, starting with your favourite one.

1 ....

2 ....

3 ....

4 ....

5 ....

6 ....

SEVEN STEPS TO SUCCESS

1 VOCABULARY

If this book belongs to you, highlight words that apply to you or tick words that you have learned; then add other words that apply to you. Customise your vocabulary so that you can talk about what interests and concerns you personally.

2 DICTIONARY

Your dictionary should have a list of verbs in it with all the perfect and imperfect tenses of irregular verbs. Make sure that you know where it is and how to use it before you go into the exam.

Use your dictionary verb list to find out the perfect tense of these four verbs:

elle lit	–	elle a lu
1 je sors	–	....
2 tu vois	–	....
3 il finit	–	....
4 nous faisons	–	....

(Answer on page 111)

3 LISTENING

When listening to a tape, don't just listen to what is said but also how it is said: in other words, the tone of voice of the speakers can tell you whether they are tired or angry, or whether their opinion is likely to be positive (enthusiastic tone of voice) or negative (bored or contemptuous tone of voice).

4 SPEAKING

Vary your tenses if at all possible: so if you are asked about your favourite hobbies, start off in the present tense, but add details which help you to use other tenses. The phrase *par exemple* will be useful for this:

> J'adore le cinéma, par exemple, samedi prochain je vais avec ma petite copine voir un film de Brad Pitt.

> Je vais souvent danser; la semaine dernière, par exemple, je suis allé(e) à une boîte de nuit en ville.

TIPS TIPS TIPS TIPS TIPS TIPS TIPS TIPS

5 READING

Practise studying the layout of any text, and use its headings, pictures, sub-titles etc. for clues to what is going on. If part of the text is in CAPITALS, or in **bold** or in *italics*, this is likely to indicate that the sentence or word is important. If it is a newspaper article, then the first and last lines often sum up what the text is about. A headline often sums this up too. Learn to work out meaning from context. For example if you see a sign at a pool which says *heures d'ouverture* next to clocks showing some times, then this is likely to mean "opening hours".

6 WRITING

When writing opinions and reasons for them, try to vary your language. In the first example below there are three alternatives to *J'aime la musique pop*. Try to make similar alternative versions of the other two sentences.

J'aime la musique pop.
- La musique pop, ça m'intéresse beaucoup.
- Mon passe-temps préféré, c'est la musique pop.
- Je trouve la musique pop passionnante.

J'aime le tennis.
- ....
- ....
- ....

J'aime la lecture.
- ....
- ....
- ....

(Answer on page 111)

7 EXAM WORK

Look for words and phrases in the letter or postcard given to you in the exam which you can re-use for your own purposes to answer the letter. If it is a question like *Qu'est-ce que tu as vu au cinéma récemment?* or *Vous restez combien de temps?* remember that your reply must be in the *je* or *nous* form, so the endings on the verb will change: *J'ai vu ...* or *Nous restons ...*

Tourism

HOLIDAYS

◆ **Foundation words**

passer	to spend (time)	la frontière	border
voyager	to travel	le pays	country
la valise	suitcase	la station de ski	ski resort
défaire sa valise	to unpack	la plage	beach
faire ses bagages	to pack	le sable	sand
faire de l'autostop	to hitch	bronzer	to sunbathe
louer	to rent, hire	le monument	monument
rencontrer	to meet		
se baigner	to bathe	un appareil photo	camera
		la carte d'identité	identity card
le congé	holiday		
le trajet	journey	quinze jours	fortnight
le tourisme	tourism	une quinzaine	fortnight
le/la touriste	tourist	tous les jours	every day
		le séjour	stay
la colonie de vacances	holiday camp	le souvenir	memory, souvenir
le gîte	holiday home	superbe	superb
le bord de la mer	seaside	une ambiance	atmosphere
la campagne	countryside	l'assurance	insurance
à l'étranger	abroad		

What are these signs telling you about?

Sens de la visite →

CHATEAU D'USSE
XVe XVIe XVIIe siècles
OUVERT au PUBLIC
du **15 MARS** au 1er NOV.

PLAGE
Location de parasols, matelas et chaises longues
Cabines, pédalos, voiliers et planches
Leçons de natation – École de voile

PIQUE-NIQUE INTERDIT SUR LA PLAGE!

SITES ET MONUMENTS HISTORIQUES
château royal
XVIe siècle
←

◆ Foundation phrases

Vous avez passé de bonnes vacances?	Did you have a good holiday?
Je suis allé à l'étranger.	I've been abroad.
Où avez-vous été?	Where did you go?
Nous sommes allés au bord de la mer.	We went to the seaside.
Je suis allé(e) en montagne avec des amis.	I went to the mountains with some friends.
Nous y avons passé une semaine.	We spent a week there.
Nous avons vu des choses intéressantes.	We saw some interesting things.
J'ai vu tous les monuments de Paris.	I saw all the monuments in Paris.
C'était superbe.	It was superb.
Où vas-tu passer tes vacances cette année?	Where are you going to spend your holidays this year?
Nous allons louer un gîte en Italie.	We're going to rent a holiday home in Italy.

MES NOTES PERSONNELLES

Mes Vacances

L'année dernière, je suis allé(e) _____

_____

avec _____

Nous y avons passé _____

Cette année, nous allons _____

_____

◆ Higher words

You might also need these words:

Add any other useful words here:

un événement	event
faire du surf	to windsurf
plonger	to dive
les festivités	festivities

....

....

....

◆ Higher phrases

Ça vaut la peine d'être vu.	It's worth seeing.
Quand est-ce que cela aura lieu?	When will that take place?

HOTELS AND YOUTH HOSTELS

◆ Foundation words

une auberge de jeunesse	youth hostel	se plaindre	to complain
un hôtel	hotel	payer	to pay
		régler	to settle
		remplir	to fill in
les arrhes	deposit	réserver	to reserve, book
la note	bill	signer	to sign
le balcon	balcony	le repas	meal
la chambre	room	le déjeuner	lunch
double	double	le dîner	dinner
pour une personne	for one person	la pension complète	full-board
simple	single	le petit déjeuner	breakfast
pour deux personnes	for two people		
de famille	for a family	la fuite	leak
avec douche	with a shower	une ampoule	bulb
avec salle de bains	with a bathroom	moderne	modern
un étage	floor	la nuit	night
le garage	garage	par personne	per person
l'hébergement (m)	accommodation	servi	served
le parking	car park	le service	service
le restaurant	restaurant	complet	full
les toilettes	toilets	compris	included
la vue	view	la fiche	form
la réception	reception	jusqu'à	until
la salle de jeux	games room	libre	free
le dortoir	dormitory	occupé	engaged
le luxe	luxury	le lit	bed
impressionnant	impressive	le drap	sheet
confirmer	to confirm	d'avance	in advance
envoyer	to send		

◆ Foundation phrases

Est-ce que je peux réserver une chambre pour la nuit du premier juillet?	Can I reserve a room for the night of July 1st?
Nous arriverons vers dix-neuf heures.	We'll arrive at about 7 pm.
Je vous enverrai un fax pour confirmer la réservation.	I'll send you a fax to confirm the reservation.
Pourriez-vous m'envoyer des arrhes?	Could you send me a deposit?
Vous avez une chambre de libre, s'il vous plaît?	Do you have a room free, please?
C'est complet.	It's full.

◆ Missing parts

*Fill in the missing part of these
half-printed signs.*

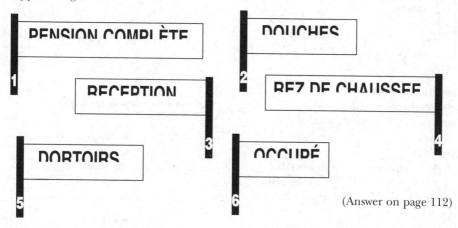

(Answer on page 112)

◆ **Foundation phrases**

Je voudrais une chambre avec vue sur les montagnes.	I'd like a room with a mountain view.
D'accord, je la prends.	Agreed, I'll take it.
J'ai réservé une chambre au nom de X.	I've reserved a room in the name of X.
Où se trouve le restaurant, s'il vous plaît?	Where's the restaurant, please?
Au rez-de-chaussée, derrière la réception.	On the ground floor, behind the reception.
Il y a un parking à l'hôtel?	Is there a car park at the hotel?
Le petit déjeuner est à quelle heure?	When is breakfast?
Le dîner est servi à partir de sept heures et demie.	Dinner is served from 7.30.
Je peux avoir ma note, s'il vous plaît?	Please can I have my bill?

Example letters to a hotel:

Madame,
suite à notre conversation téléphonique, je confirme ma réservation d'une chambre pour deux personnes, pour la nuit du quinze avril. Voulez-vous m'envoyer la liste des prix et votre brochure?
Je vous prie d'agréer, Madame, l'expression de mes sentiments les meilleurs.

Madame, Monsieur,
je voudrais réserver une chambre double, du trente juillet au dix août. Pouvez-vous confirmer cette réservation, s'il vous plaît?
Je vous prie d'agréer, Madame, Monsieur, l'expression de mes sentiments distingués.

◆ **Higher words**

You might also need these words:

		Add any other useful words here:
les aménagements	facilities	
critiquer	to criticise	....
la TVA	VAT	
la demi-pension	bed, breakfast and evening meal	....
scandaleux	disgraceful	....

◆ **Higher phrases**

Je voulais une chambre avec balcon. — I wanted a room with a balcony.
Je voudrais me plaindre au directeur. — I want to complain to the manager.
Les aménagements sont scandaleux. — The facilities are a disgrace.
J'ai passé un très bon séjour ici. — I've had a really good stay here.

CAMPING

◆ **Foundation words**

la tente	tent	la lampe de poche	torch
le sac de couchage	sleeping bag	un ouvre-boîte	tin opener
le canif	penknife	un ouvre-bouteille	bottle opener
le bloc sanitaire	wash facilities	le tire-bouchon	corkscrew
la caravane	caravan	la pile	battery
le camping	campsite	une allumette	match
un emplacement	pitch		

◆ **Foundation phrases**

Vous avez de la place pour deux personnes? — Do you have room for two people?

Ça coûte combien par nuit pour une tente? — How much does it cost per night for a tent?

Est-ce que le camping est bien aménagé? — Is the site well-equipped?

Read these campsite notices.

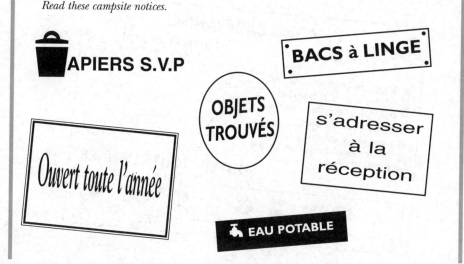

APIERS S.V.P

BACS à LINGE

OBJETS TROUVÉS

s'adresser à la réception

Ouvert toute l'année

EAU POTABLE

◆ Higher words

You might also need these words:

le feu de camp	camp fire
les ordures	rubbish
l'extinction des lumières	"lights out"
le réchaud	camp stove
l'ombre (f)	shade
le dépôt de butane	calor gas shop
la prise de courant	electric socket

Add any other useful words here:

....

....

....

....

....

....

◆ Higher phrases

On peut louer un matelas pneumatique?	Can you hire an airbed?
Où devons-nous dresser notre tente?	Where should we pitch our tent?
Est-ce que les feux de camp sont permis?	Are camp fires allowed?
Je préférerais un emplacement à l'ombre.	I'd prefer a place in the shade.

What's on offer at this campsite?

CAMPING CARAVANING

14430 DOZULÉ   TEL. 03 81 24 77 45

■ 3 km de la mer
■ Pêche sur la propriété
■ Produits fermiers naturels sur place
■ Terrain de boules
■ Jeux pour enfants
■ Douches chaudes et froides
■ École de voile

OUVERT TOUTE L'ANNÉE

SEVEN STEPS TO SUCCESS

1 VOCABULARY

If you like using computers and you have one at home, set up your own vocabulary database, which you can regularly update. This can be by topic, alphabetical, French-English or English-French, or whatever you choose.

Set yourself little tests and games on the computer, which you can save and use for revision later. You could, for example, write out some key phrases with words missing, which you have below, and which you need to cut and paste to complete the sentences. Your screen might look like this:

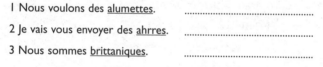

1. Nous arriverons --- dix neuf ---
2. Nous --- une chambre avec --- de bain
3. Le petit --- est --- dans la chambre?

préférons, servi, vers, déjeuner, heures, salle

2 DICTIONARY

Your dictionary helps not just with meanings but also with spellings.
Use your dictionary to correct the spellings of the underlined words in these sentences:

1 Nous voulons des <u>alumettes</u>. ....

2 Je vais vous envoyer des <u>ahrres</u>. ....

3 Nous sommes <u>brittaniques</u>. ....

(Answer on page 112)

3 LISTENING

If your school has a fast copier, you may be able to give your teacher a blank tape and ask if you can have a copy of a suitable French tape – you can then practise listening at home. You may be able to have a copy of the tapes that accompany your course book if the school has cleared that with the publishers for private home study.

4 SPEAKING

The higher role play in particular will expect you to cope with "unpredictable" events or problems. The trick is to try to think in advance what these problems might be and how you will react. Here are some examples:
1. If you are told you can only afford to spend 200 francs on a room, then you may well be offered a room at more than that price. Therefore, you cannot just

say *Très bien, merci*. You need to think about how to say it is too expensive, and ask for a cheaper room, or else find another hotel.

2. If you are told that you booked a room by phone, then the receptionist may tell you that there is no record of your call. Therefore, you need to ask if they have one available anyway, or if they can recommend somewhere else.

3. If you are told to book a room for the night with a shower, be prepared in case they only have a room with a bath.

5 READING

When you are looking for an answer in a longish text, look through for the likely word. For example, if the question wants to know *Où se trouve l'hôtel?* look out for words or phrases such as *près de* or *à côté de*.

What kind of French words might you be looking for if the question asks:

1 Quand le camping est-il fermé? ....

2 Où est-ce qu'on peut manger? ....

3 Qu'est-ce qu'on peut faire dans l'auberge de jeunesse?...

(Answer on page 112)

6 WRITING

Remember to use appropriate words in a letter:

INFORMAL	FORMAL
tu (ton, ta, tes)	vous (votre vos)
cher, chère	Monsieur, Madame
s'il te plaît	s'il vous plaît
amitiés	Je vous prie d'agréer, Madame/Monsieur, l'expression de mes sentiments les meilleurs.

7 EXAM WORK

You need to complete all the tasks the question paper asks you to, since a lot of marks go on completing the task set. However good your French is, if you do not cover all the points you have to, or answer all the questions set, you will lose marks – tick them off on your question paper once you have answered them, especially in the writing paper.

Social Activities

SOCIALISING

◆ **Foundation words**

bonjour	hello	le/la camarade	friend
salut	hi!	le/la correspondant(e)	penfriend
accueillant	welcoming	ça dépend	it depends
bonsoir	good evening	d'accord	OK
ça va	I'm fine	certainement	certainly
enchanté	pleased to meet you	désolé	very sorry
à bientôt	see you soon	il faut	it's necessary
à demain	till tomorrow	impossible	impossible
à samedi	see you on Saturday	je m'excuse	I'm sorry
à tout à l'heure	see you in a bit	je veux bien	with pleasure
au revoir	goodbye	malheureusement	unfortunately
bonne nuit	good night	peut-être	perhaps
		possible	possible
la boum	party	présenter	to introduce
la fête	party	la raison	reason
la surprise-partie	party	ravi	delighted
accepter	to accept	refuser	to refuse
accompagner	to go with	regretter	to regret
connaître	to know	rencontrer	to meet
décider	to decide	saluer	to wave
déranger	to disturb		

See page 59 for more about trips.

◆ **Foundation phrases**

Je te présente mon frère, Alain.	This is my brother, Alain.
Comment allez-vous?	How are you?
Voici mon correspondant français.	This is my French penfriend.
Tu vas rencontrer toute ma famille.	You're going to meet all of my family.
Je ne connais pas Claire.	I don't know Claire.
J'accepte ton invitation avec plaisir.	I accept your invitation with pleasure.
Malheureusement, je ne pourrai pas venir.	Unfortunately, I won't be able to come.
Je regrette mais je dois rester avec ma petite sœur.	I'm sorry but I have to stay at home with my little sister.
C'est dommage!	It's a shame!
Ah, tu es très gentil!	Ah, that's very nice of you!
Quelle bonne idée!	What a good idea!

SPECIAL EVENTS AND FESTIVALS

◆ Foundation words

félicitations	congratulations	le premier janvier	January 1st
Joyeux Noël	Happy Christmas	le premier mai	May 1st
un anniversaire	birthday	le quatorze juillet	July 14th
bon anniversaire	Happy birthday	le onze novembre	November 11th
bonne année	Happy New Year	le vingt-cinq décembre	December 25th
avoir lieu	to take place		
le cadeau	present	religieux	religious
la carte	card	la religion	religion
la fête	holiday, festival	dieu	god
important	important	chrétien	christian
le Nouvel An	New Year	protestant	protestant
Pâques	Easter	catholique	catholic
se passer	to happen	juif	jewish
la sorte de	sort of	musulman	muslim
spécial	special	sikh	sikh
étonner	to surprise	hindou	hindu
		bouddhiste	buddist

MES NOTES PERSONNELLES

Les Dates

Mon anniversaire _____

_____

L'anniversaire de _____

_____

_____

Des dates importantes pour moi

_____

_____

_____

_____

_____

SOCIAL ACTIVITIES

◆ Foundation words

agréable	pleasant	prochain	next
s'amuser	to have fun	remercier	to thank
avec plaisir	with pleasure	revenir	to return
bienvenu(e)	welcome	cet après-midi	this afternoon
bon voyage!	have a good journey!	ce soir	this evening
		entendu	OK
bon week-end	have a good weekend!	le rendez-vous	meeting
		prendre rendez-vous	to arrange to meet
bonne chance	good luck		
heureux/heureuse	happy	(se) rencontrer	to meet (each other)
l'hospitalité	hospitality		
une invitation	invitation	la semaine	week
montrer	to show	se voir	to meet
passer	to spend (time)		

◆ Foundation phrases

Bienvenu(e) chez nous.	Welcome to our house.
Tu as fait bon voyage?	Did you have a good journey?
Je vais te montrer ta chambre.	I'll show you your room.
Tu es fatigué(e)?	Are you tired?
Merci beaucoup pour votre hospitalité.	Thank you very much for your hospitality.
Vous êtes très gentils.	You are very kind.
Je me suis bien amusé(e).	I've had a lot of fun.
J'espère que tu viendras bientôt chez moi.	I hope you'll come soon to my house.
C'était un séjour formidable.	It was a great visit.
Ça te va?	Does that suit you?
A quelle heure est-ce qu'on se rencontre?	When shall we meet?
A midi, ça te va?	At midday, is that OK for you?
Où est-ce qu'on se voit?	Where shall we meet?
Je t'attendrai à l'arrêt d'autobus.	I'll wait for you at the bus stop.

◆ Higher words

You might also need these words:

le plaisir	pleasure
se disputer	to quarrel
exprès	on purpose
ça vaut le coup	it's well worth it

Add any other useful words here:

....

....

◆ Higher phrases

Tout le plaisir est pour moi.	The pleasure's mine.

SEVEN STEPS TO SUCCESS

1 VOCABULARY

A simple way to test yourself quickly on words you have learned is to chop them in half and write them down in two lists. Later you try to put the words back together again.

Put these chopped-up words back together again:

anniv	pondant	....
accom	eusement	....
malheur	able	....
corres	pagner	....
renc	ontrer	....
agré	ersaire	....

(Answer on page 112)

2 DICTIONARY

Set phrases are often difficult to translate, because you don't translate them word for word. If you want to say "it doesn't matter" and you look up "matter", don't end up choosing the wrong word. The dictionary will usually give you the whole phrase.

Look up the underlined words in a dictionary to see if the whole phrase is given:

1 <u>Happy</u> birthday!

2 You're <u>welcome</u>!

3 Bad <u>luck</u>!

3 LISTENING

See if what you are listening for is presented in two different ways, so that even if you don't understand one phrase, the sense of the whole passage is clear.

For example:

1 Je n'ai rien contre, en fait je suis tout à fait d'accord.

2 Bienvenue! C'est un plaisir de te voir!

3 Je ne pourrai pas venir, c'est impossible pour moi.

4 SPEAKING

In real life you can help get your message across with miming and pointing: that will not do in an exam that is being recorded on cassette! Try not to miss out what you think you can't say in the role-play: you need to get round words or phrases you have forgotten and did not look up in the dictionary. For example, use *Bonne nuit!* if you can't remember *Dors bien!*

5 READING

Read the questions before you read the text: you then know what kind of information you are looking out for and will read the text with a definite purpose in mind. Use the dictionary on the questions as well, if necessary, so that you are sure you understand what you are looking for. A list of question words can be found on page 109, and a list of rubrics is provided on page 12.

6 WRITING

If you can use a wordprocessor, then write some of your homeworks this way. When you get your work back, enter the teacher's corrections into your original version that you saved: this is a good way of doing corrections to learn from your mistakes, and you can print out a set of model letters from which to revise as the exam gets closer. Coursework presented this way may also look much better.

7 EXAM WORK

Always re-read your answers, and the questions, in any time you have left at the end of the exam. A surprising number of marks are lost because candidates misread things like "where" for "when", or because the answer is unclear.

International World

◆ **Foundation words**

l'Afrique	Africa	l'Espagne	Spain
américain	American	espagnol	Spanish
l'Amérique	America	la Finlande	Finland
les Etats-Unis	United States	finlandais	Finnish
le Canada	Canada	la France	France
le Québec	Quebec	français	French
		la Grèce	Greece
l'Angleterre	England	grec	Greek
anglais	English	la Hollande/	Holland
l'Ecosse	Scotland	les Pays-Bas	
écossais	Scottish	hollandais	Dutch
le Pays de Galles	Wales	l'Italie	Italy
gallois	Welsh	italien	Italian
l'Irlande	Ireland	le Portugal	Portugal
irlandais	Irish	portugais	Portuguese
		la Suède	Sweden
l'Allemagne	Germany	suédois	Swedish
allemand	German	la Suisse	Switzerland
l'Autriche	Austria	suisse	Swiss
autrichien	Austrian		
la Belgique	Belgium	la Tamise	Thames
belge	Belgian	les Nations Unies	United Nations
le Danemark	Denmark	L'Europe	Europe
danois	Danish		

◆ **Foundation phrases**

J'ai passé les vacances de Noël au Canada.	I spent the Christmas holidays in Canada.
J'aimerais aller aux Etats-Unis.	I'd like to go to the United States.
Je n'ai jamais été en Suisse.	I've never been to Switzerland.
Mon père est écossais.	My father is Scottish.
J'ai un correspondant danois.	I've got a Danish penfriend.

> **MES NOTES PERSONNELLES**
> *La Nationalité*
>
> Je suis né(e) en _____
>
> Je parle _____
>
> Mon père est _____ Ma mère est _____

WORLD ISSUES

◆ Foundation words

une élection	election	la sécurité	safety
la monarchie	monarchy	le trou	hole
le Premier Ministre	Prime Minister		
le Président	President	le meurtre	murder
la reine	Queen	le voleur	thief
une exposition	exhibition	le voyou	hooligan
les festivités	festivities	un avertissement	warning
le gouvernement	government	disparu	disappeared
le siècle	century	éviter	to avoid
le sondage	survey, poll	la guerre	war
le Tiers Monde	Thrid World	le monde	world
		la sécheresse	drought
attaquer	to attack	détruire	to destroy
la crise	crisis	diminuer	to reduce
empêcher	to prevent	disparaître	to disappear
enlever	to kidnap	les dégâts	damage
un évènement	event	une inondation	flood
la grève	strike	un incendie	fire
la manifestation	demonstration	la pollution	pollution

◆ Higher words

You might also need these words:

		Add any other useful words here:
le racisme	racism	
la pauvreté	poverty	....
la pluie acide	acid rain	
le vol à l'étalage	shop lifting	....

◆ Higher phrases

Le racisme est un grand problème pour l'avenir.   Racism is a big problem for the future.

◆ Definitions

What words from this section are being described here?

1 Une dispute entre deux pays.
2 Beaucoup de flammes; il faut appeler les sapeurs-pompiers.
3 Il n'y a pas d'eau et le temps est très sec.
4 Il y a trop de pluie et d'eau.

(Answer on page 112)

THE WEATHER

◆ Foundation words

le temps	weather	chaud	hot
le climat	climate	le brouillard	fog
le degré	degree	la brume	mist
la météo	weather forecast	couvert	overcast
la température	temperature	sombre	dark
variable	changeable	froid	cold
les prévisions	predictions		
rapidement	quickly	geler	to freeze
		la glace	ice
faible	weak	le verglas	black ice
fort	strong	neiger	to snow
léger	light	la neige	snow
mauvais	bad	la tempête	storm
meilleur	better	un orage	storm
rare	rare	le tonnerre	thunder
le soleil	sun	pleuvoir	to rain
une éclaircie	sunny spell	pluvieux	rainy
ensoleillé	sunny	la pluie	rain
agréable	pleasant	humide	wet
beau	fine	le nuage	cloud
la chaleur	heat	le vent	wind

◆ Foundation phrases

Aujourd'hui, il fait froid.	It's cold today.
Il pleut.	It's raining.
Il fait du vent.	It's windy.
Il fait très beau!	What nice weather!
Quel temps fera-t-il demain?	What will the weather be like tomorrow?
Voici la météo pour demain.	Here's the weather forecast for tomorrow.
L'après-midi, il fera mauvais.	In the afternoon, the weather will be bad.
Il fera chaud plus tard.	It will be hot later.
Normalement, il fait beau en été.	Normally, the weather is good in summer.

◆ Weather symbols

Draw a weather symbol for each phrase.

| Il pleut. | Il y a du soleil. | Il fait froid. | Il neige. | Il y a de l'orage. |

◆ Higher words

You might also need these words:

prévoir	to predict
dégagé	clear
doux	mild
une averse	shower
la grêle	hail

Add any other useful words here:

....

....

....

◆ Higher phrases

On dirait qu'il va pleuvoir.	It looks like rain.
J'espère qu'il ne pleuvra pas.	I hope it'll stay dry.
A cause du mauvais temps.	Due to the bad weather.
Il pleuvait à verse.	It was pouring down.

What's the weather going to be like?

Météo ◑

Le grand soleil doit effectuer son retour avec un ciel dégagé et bleu sur la plupart des régions.

Par endroits, cependant, la patience sera de mise, le temps pour les brumes et brouillards matinaux de se dissiper. En revanche, sur la Bretagne et le Pays basque, les nuages seront assez nombreux dès le matin.

Au fil des heures, des nuages atteindront aussi les Pays de la Loire et la Normandie. Dans la journée, après une nuit très fraîche sur le quart nord-est, la température variera de 12 à 20° du nord au sud. Les vents, près de la Méditerranée, faibliront dans l'après-midi.

sud-sud-ouest à sud-ouest modérés, température maximale de l'ordre de 16°.

Prévisions valables jusqu'au 20 avril :

Dimanche et lundi : temps variable avec de nombreux nuages et brumes en début de journée, puis aggravation au cours de la journée avec des ondées localement orageuses. Les orages, isolés dimanche, seront plus fréquents lundi et les pluies plus fortes. Vents de sud-ouest modérés devenant assez forts lundi. Températures douces pour la saison. Température maximale 18 à 20°.

Mardi et mercredi : temps plus frais avec alternance d'éclaircies et de passages nuageux accompagnés d'averses. Vent d'ouest à sud-ouest modérés à assez forts. Températures en baisse.

THE NATURAL ENVIRONMENT

◆ Foundation words

la marée	tide	le champ	field
la côte	coast	la ferme	farm
le rocher	rock	la fleur	flower
la falaise	cliff	la feuille	leaf
la rivière	river	la terre	earth
le fleuve	river	la lune	moon
le paysage	landscape	une étoile	star
la campagne	countryside	la vallée	valley
un arbre	tree	tuer	to kill
le bois	wood	la chasse	hunt
la forêt	forest		

◆ Foundation phrases

J'habite près d'une rivière.	I live near a river.
Ce n'est pas loin de la côte.	It's not far from the coast.

◆ Higher words

You might also need these words:

raide	steep
le ruisseau	stream
paisible	peaceful
le pré	meadow

Add any other useful words here:

....

....

....

◆ Higher phrases

Dans ma région le paysage est très plat.	The countryside in my region is very flat.

What are these stickers about?

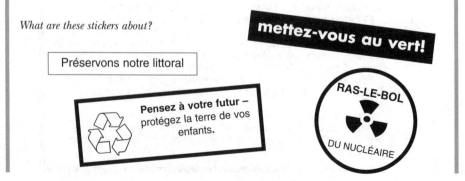

Préservons notre littoral

mettez-vous au vert!

Pensez à votre futur –
protégez la terre de vos
enfants.

RAS-LE-BOL

DU NUCLÉAIRE

SEVEN STEPS TO SUCCESS

1 **VOCABULARY**
Some people learn best by seeing words written down, others like to hear them. It might help you to record words and phrases onto a tape, so that you have to read them out, and then you can listen to them, perhaps on a walkman:
• Record a French word or phrase.
• Leave a short gap (three seconds).
• Record the English meaning.
• When you listen to the tape later, say the English word in the gap.
• Then listen to see if you were right.

2 **DICTIONARY**
A good dictionary will help you with proper names as well as other aspects of language. So you can look up "London" and find *Londres*. Most names of towns remain the same of course, so Paris is *Paris* and Madrid is *Madrid*. Your dictionary may even have a list of countries.
Use your dictionary to find the French for:

1 Dover ....

2 Edinburgh ....

3 Brittany ....

4 Brussels ....

(Answer on page 112)

3 **LISTENING**
Listen to any background noises on the tape for clues as to meaning: the sound of traffic, the ringing of a phone, the sound of a door opening can all contribute to your understanding of what you hear.

4 **SPEAKING**
If varying the tenses is difficult because the topic is limited, use the phrase *par exemple*. This will enable you to introduce another tense: *La pollution est un gros problème. Par exemple, la semaine dernière, j'ai remarqué ...*
Make up two more examples from these starting phrases:

1 Le climat en Grande-Bretagne est très variable. Par exemple

....

2 J'aime visiter d'autres pays. Par exemple

....

5 READING

Sometimes in addition to the French words, there may be extra help in the form of pictures, photos, cartoons, symbols. These might give you a clue to help you answer questions.

6 WRITING

Sometimes you write about things which have already happened, and for this you use the perfect tense. Try to "scatter" a few opinions or descriptions into your sentences to enable you to use the imperfect tense as well. For example:

J'ai vu un incendie dans le bois. C'était très dangereux.

Nous avons campé dans un champ qui se trouvait près d'une rivière.

Extend these sentences in the same way, and ask your teacher to check them:

1 Mes parents ont loué un gîte à la campagne ....

2 Nous sommes restés à la maison parce que ....

7 EXAM WORK

Your handwriting can make a difference between the examiner being able to tell what you mean or not. Look carefully at what you have written. If anything is unclear, cross it out and redo it. Unlike many subjects, you rarely have to write very much in French, so take your time and do it neatly, printing if necessary.

Home Town

◆ **Foundation words**

la boutique	shop	nombreux	numerous
la banque	bank	construire	to build
la cathédrale	cathedral	donner sur	to overlook
le château	castle	le boulevard	avenue
le commissariat	police station	jumelé	twinned
une église	church		
un hôtel de ville	town hall	la région	region
la mairie	town hall	la ville	town
un hôpital	hospital	le village	village
un hôtel	hotel	la banlieue	suburb
un office de tourisme	tourist office	le centre-ville	town centre
le syndicat d'initiative	information office	la place	square
		le port	port
la poste	post office	la rivière	river
la zone piétonne	pedestrian precinct	le jardin public	park, gardens
		l'industrie (f)	industry
la bibliothèque	library	les remparts	city walls
animé	lively	le monument	monument
le bruit	noise	la fontaine	fountain
calme	quiet	une horloge	clock
historique	historical	le pont	bridge
important	big, important	le banc	bench
industriel	industrial		
		le bâtiment	building
le kilomètre	kilometre	un habitant	inhabitant
loin de	far from	le passage clouté	zebra crossing
proche	nearby		
près (d'ici)	near (here)		
situé	situated		

See page 88 for shops.

◆ **Foundation phrases**

La ville n'est pas belle mais elle est intéressante.
The town isn't attractive but it's interesting.

On peut visiter un vieux château.
You can visit an old castle.

C'est une région industrielle dans le sud de l'Angleterre.
It's an industrial region in the south of England.

◆ **Higher words**
You might also need these words:

la clinique   hospital
le cimetière   cemetery
la rocade   bypass

Add any other useful words here:

....

....

◆ **Higher phrases**

Ce qui manque, c'est un joli jardin public.   What's missing is a nice park.

FINDING THE WAY

◆ **Foundation words**

après	after	en face de	opposite
une autoroute	motorway	le feu	traffic lights
avant	before	jusqu'à	as far as
au bout de	at the end of	là-bas	down there
le carrefour	crossroads	monter	to go up
la carte	map	où	where
le coin	corner	passer	to cross, pass
continuer	to continue	à pied	on foot
à côté de	next to	le plan	town plan
demander	to ask	prendre	to take
derrière	behind	prochain	next
devant	in front of	puis	then
descendre	to go down	le rond-point	roundabout
les directions	directions	la route	road
la distance	distance	la rue	street
à droite	on the right	tourner	to turn
à gauche	on the left	toutes directions	all routes
tout droit	straight on	traverser	to cross
entre	between		

◆ **Foundation phrases**

Pour aller au syndicat d'initiative, s'il vous plaît?   How do I get to the tourist office, please?

Continuez tout droit.   Go straight on.

Prenez la première rue à gauche.   Take the first road on the left.

Tournez à droite aux feux.   Turn right at the traffic lights.

Allez jusqu'à l'hôpital.   Go as far as the hospital.

Ce n'est pas loin.   It's not far.

C'est à cinq minutes à pied.   It's five minutes on foot.

◆ **Higher words**

You might also need these words:

suivre   to follow
la rue latérale   side road
s'égarer   to get lost
la visite guidée   guided tour

Add any other useful words here:

....

....

....

....

◆ **Higher phrases**

Où est-ce que je peux me renseigner?   Where can I make enquiries?

Je me suis égaré.   I've got lost.

◆ **Town grid**

Answer the clues by writing the words across the grid.
What is the building reading down from the arrow?

1 Ici on voit un film.

2 **i** = l'........ de tourisme.

3 Le contraire de «proche».

4 Lille, par exemple.

5 La mairie = l'........ de ville.

6 On y va pour prier.

7 Les PTT.

(Answer on page 112)

SEVEN STEPS TO SUCCESS

1 **VOCABULARY**
Although you need to learn the gender of words, there are some endings that can help you.
Look back at words in this section, and write down the gender these endings show:

1 banque, boutique   ....

2 direction, région   ....

3 bâtiment, monument   ....

(Answer on page 112)

2 **DICTIONARY**
Where possible, stick to words you already know when speaking and writing. Using the dictionary a lot will take up too much time and could tempt you to try and say things you cannot do yet. Play safe!! Learning words in context rather then in isolation helps. Try to learn the phrases given in this book as well as the lists of vocabulary.

3 **LISTENING**
The answers to the questions are almost always in the same order on the tape as the questions, so if you missed a question on the first hearing, you know where to listen carefully the second time.

4 **SPEAKING**
You do not have to be totally truthful in your answers! For example, if you live opposite an insurance building and you can't say that, then in the oral exam you can say you live near a church or a bank. Nobody will check up on you! By inventing, you can also give more interesting answers, so instead of just saying you like TV and pop music (which is what a lot of other exam candidates will probably say), be more original!

5 **READING**
Look carefully at any examples of how to answer a question that are given to you, as they will tell you exactly how you should show your understanding of the text. The example may be easier to understand than the instructions to the question!

6 WRITING

If you feel confident that you can write longish sentences, then that will be to your advantage. For example, don't write *J'habite à Exeter. C'est une belle ville* but join it into one sentence such as *J'habite à Exeter qui est une belle ville.*

Practise making these pairs of sentences into just one longer sentence, using each of the words in the box once only.

1 Il y a beaucoup de magasins. On peut acheter des articles bon marché.

....

2 Il y a beaucoup de choses à voir. Vous vous intéressez aux musées.

....

3 En hiver, il fait souvent froid. La ville est située en montagne.

....

| si |
| où |
| parce que |

(Answer on page 112)

7 EXAM WORK

At GCSE level, nobody expects you to speak or write as perfectly as a French person. If you are getting the message across in a way that a French person could understand, however many mistakes there are in it, then you may get some credit. It is only when a French person could not tell what you mean that you are not given any credit at all. But aim to get your spelling and grammar as accurate as possible: that will get you better marks, particularly at higher tier.

Shopping and Eating

SHOPPING

◆ Foundation words

le magasin	shop	fermé	closed
l'alimentation (f)	food	fermer	to close
la poissonnerie	fishmongers	jusqu'à	until
la boucherie	butcher's	ouvert	open
la charcuterie	pork butcher's	à partir de	from
la boulangerie	baker's	la fermeture	closing
la confiserie	sweet shop	l'ouverture	opening
la pâtisserie	cake shop	le rayon	shelf
une épicerie	grocer's	la vitrine	shop window
		faire du lèche-vitrines	to window shop
le marché	market	garantir	guarantee
le centre commercial	shopping centre	rembourser	to refund
un hypermarché	hypermarket	le chariot	shopping trolley
le supermarché	supermarket	le libre-service	self-service
le grand magasin	department store	le produit	product
		en promotion	on offer
la papeterie	stationer's, newsagent's	en réclame	on special offer
		le reçu	receipt
la bijouterie	jeweller's	le sac à main	handbag
la librairie	bookshop	en vente	on sale
le bureau de tabac	tobacconist's	le comptoir	counter
la parfumerie	perfume shop		
la pharmacie	chemist's		

See page 83 for places in town.

◆ Shop talk

Match up the speech bubbles with the places they might be said.

1 Il reste des baguettes?

2 Je vais prendre trois tranches de jambon.

3 Pour envoyer une lettre en Irlande, ça coûte combien?

4 Le thon est très bon aujourd'hui.

5 Qu'est-ce que vous prenez comme dessert?

6 Je voudrais changer des chèques de voyage.

A **La poste**

B **Le restaurant**

C **La poissonnerie**

D **La boulangerie**

E **La boucherie**

F **La banque**

(Answer on page 112)

◆ **Foundation phrases**

Où est la boucherie?	Where's the butcher's?
Il y a une pharmacie ici?	Is there a chemist's here?
Où est-ce que je pourrais acheter un peigne?	Where could I buy a comb?
La pharmacie ouvre à quelle heure?	When does the chemist's open?
Elle est fermée jusqu'à deux heures.	It's closed until two o'clock.
Le magasin est ouvert jusqu'à neuf heures du soir.	The shop is open until nine pm.
Vous fermez à quelle heure?	When do you close?
On est fermé entre midi et une heure.	We're closed between twelve noon and one o'clock.

What are these shop signs about?

◆ **Higher words**

You might also need these words:

la fermeture annuelle	business holidays
échanger	to exchange
disponible	available
un acompte	deposit

Add any other useful words here:

....

....

....

◆ **Higher phrases**

Je voudrais échanger ce sac à main.	I'd like to exchange this handbag.
Il reste des pommes?	Are there any apples left?

FOOD AND DRINK

◆ **Foundation words**

le légume	vegetable	le pamplemousse	grapefruit
la carotte	carrot	la pêche	peach
le champignon	mushroom	la poire	pear
le chou	cabbage	la pomme	apple
le chou de Bruxelles	Brussel sprout	la prune	plum
le chou-fleur	cauliflower	le raisin	grapes
la courgette	courgette		
les crudités	raw vegetables	la viande	meat
un haricot vert	French bean	l'agneau	lamb
la laitue	lettuce	le bifteck	beefsteak
un oignon	onion	du boeuf	beef
les petits pois	peas	la côtelette	chop
la pomme de terre	potato	une entrecôte	steak
la salade	salad, lettuce	un escargot	snail
la tomate	tomato	un hamburger	hamburger
un artichaut	artichoke	le jambon	ham
le concombre	cucumber	le pâté	pâté
		du porc	pork
le fruit	fruit	le saucisson	slicing sausage
un abricot	apricot	le steak	steak
un ananas	pineapple	le veau	veal
la banane	banana	la saucisse	sausage
la cerise	cherry		
le citron	lemon	le canard	duck
la fraise	strawberry	la dinde	turkey
la framboise	raspberry	le poulet	chicken
une orange	orange	le poisson	fish

le crabe	crab
les fruits de mer	seafood
la moule	mussel
le thon	tuna
le croissant	croissant
le dessert	dessert
un éclair	eclair
le gâteau	cake
la glace	ice cream
le biscuit	biscuit
la pâtisserie	cakes, pastry
la tarte	pie
le yaourt	yogurt
boire	to drink
la boisson	drink
le café	coffee (black)
le café-crème	white coffee
au lait	with milk
le thé	tea
le chocolat chaud	hot chocolate

l'alcool	alcohol
la bière	beer
le rosé	rosé wine
le vin	wine
l'eau minérale (f)	mineral water
le lait	milk
le coca (-cola)	coke
le jus de fruit	fruit juice
la limonade	lemonade
un orangina	fizzy orange
le potage	soup
le casse-croûte	snack
un œuf	egg
un œuf à la coque	hard boiled egg
les pâtes	pasta
la pizza	pizza
le plat	dish
rôti	roasted
la sauce	sauce, gravy
les spaghettis	spaghetti
le toast	toast

◆ **Food wordsearch**

Can you find 16 words from this section in the wordsearch?
The words can be across or down, backwards or forwards or diagonal.

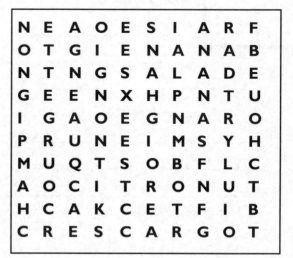

```
N E A O E S I A R F
O T G I E N A N A B
N T N G S A L A D E
G E E N X H P N T U
I G A O E G N A R O
P R U N E I M S Y H
M U Q T S O B F L C
A O C I T R O N U T
H C A K C E T F I B
C R E S C A R G O T
```

(Answer on page 112)

le pain	bread	bien cuit	well done
la tartine	slice of bread, butter and jam	appétissant	appetising
		désagréable	unpleasant
la baguette	French loaf	le bistro	café
le bonbon	sweet	bon appétit	enjoy your meal
les céréales	cereals	doux	sweet
les chips	crisps	sucré	sweet
le chocolat	chocolate	salé	salty
la crème	cream	épais	thick
la crêpe	pancake	gras	fatty
la farine	flour	grillé	grilled
les frites	chips	la vapeur	steam
le fromage	cheese	le pique-nique	picnic
végétarien	vegetarian	le plat cuisiné	pre-made meal
		la recette	recipe
chaud	warm, hot	le self	self service
froid	cold	le souper	supper
mûr	ripe	délicieux	delicious
sauvage	wild	désirer	to want
saignant	rare	manger	to eat
à point	medium	prendre	to take

MES NOTES PERSONNELLES

Manger et Boire

J'aime beaucoup _____

_____

_____

Je n'aime pas _____

_____

_____

Mon plat préféré, c'est _____

_____

Au petit déjeuner, je mange _____

_____

et je bois _____

◆ Foundation phrases

Vous aimez le porc?	Do you like pork?
Moi, je préfère le bœuf.	I prefer beef.
Mon copain est végétarien.	My friend's a vegetarian.
Je déteste les oignons.	I hate onions.
Nous mangeons beaucoup de fromage chez nous.	We eat a lot of cheese at home.
Nous buvons normalement de la limonade.	We normally drink lemonade.
Merci, ça va bien comme ça.	No thank you, that's enough.
C'était délicieux mais j'ai très bien mangé.	It was delicious but I'm full.

What's on offer here?

◆ Foundation words

une assiette	plate	passer	to pass
le bol	bowl	le beurre	butter
la cafetière	coffee-pot	la confiture	jam
le couteau	knife	l'huile (f)	oil
la cuiller	spoon	le miel	honey
la fourchette	fork	la moutarde	mustard
la poêle	frying pan	le poivre	pepper
la soucoupe	saucer	le sel	salt
la tasse	cup	le sucre	sugar
le verre	glass	le vinaigre	vinegar

◆ Foundation phrases

Excusez-moi, mais je n'ai pas de couteau.	Excuse me, but I haven't got a knife.
Passe-moi le poivre, s'il te plaît.	Pass me the pepper, please.
Vous avez du sucre?	Do you have any sugar?
Je voudrais encore un peu de confiture, s'il vous plaît.	I'd like a little more jam, please.

◆ Higher words

You might also need these words:

sentir	to smell
goûter	to taste
une infusion	herbal tea
la gaufre	waffle
les cacahuètes	peanuts

Add any other useful words here:

....

....

....

....

....

....

....

....

◆ Higher phrases

Cela a un goût d'ail.	This tastes of garlic.
Cela ne me convient pas.	That doesn't agree with me.
A consommer de préférence avant ...	Best before ...

TES
LLES

nts

A l'école, je porte

_____

_____

Le soir, quand je sors

_____

_____

il fait chaud, je mets

_____

_____

ements préférés sont

_____

_____

vords

size	lourd	heavy
size (for shoes)	moyen	medium
nylon	étroi	narrow
cotton	large	wide
leather	rayé	striped
wool	léger	light
colour	malheureusement	unfortunately
short	prendre	to take
long		

ases

est belle, n'est-ce pas?	That dress is beautiful, isn't it?
ures sont trop chères.	These shoes are too expensive.
prends ce pantalon.	Fine, I'll take this pair of trousers.
hose de moins cher?	Do you have anything less expensive?
erméable en coton.	I'd like a cotton mac.
ne paire de baskets.	I'd like a pair of trainers.
Quelle pointure?	What size?
hemisier en rouge?	Have you got this blouse in red?
Quelle taille?	What size?
cles d'oreilles pour ma belle-sœur.	I'm going to buy some earrings for my sister-in-law.
me chose en bleu?	Do you have the same thing in blue?

RESTAURANTS AND CAFÉS

◆ Foundation words

choisir	to choose	le riz	rice
apporter	to bring	le sandwich	sandwich
donner	to give	sans	without
pour commencer	to start	la soupe	soup
vouloir	to want	la vanille	vanilla
commander	to order	le repas	meal
prendre	to have, take	le restaurant	restaurant
		le serveur	waiter
la bouteille	bottle	la serveuse	waitress
la carte	menu		
le croque-monsieur	toasted cheese-ham sandwich	une addition	bill
		compris	included
demi	half	en sus	on top
une omelette	omelette	une erreur	mistake
le parfum	flavour	le service	service

◆ Foundation phrases

S'il vous plaît!	Waiter/Waitress!
Pour commencer, je prends les crudités.	To start with, I'll have the raw vegetables.
Ensuite je voudrais une omelette.	Then I'd like an omelette.
Comme dessert, je prendrai une glace.	For dessert, I'll have an ice cream.
Qu'est-ce que vous avez comme sandwichs?	What sorts of sandwiches have you got?
Un sandwich au jambon.	A ham sandwich.
Comment voulez-vous le steak?	How would you like the steak?
Bien cuit, s'il vous plaît.	Well done, please.
Qu'est-ce que c'est exactement une assiette anglaise?	What exactly is "une assiette anglaise"?
Je prends le menu à cent dix francs.	I'll have the 110 franc menu.
Comme plat principal, je voudrais le steak avec des petits pois.	For the main course, I'd like the steak and peas.
Qu'est-ce que vous recommandez?	What do you recommend?
Monsieur, l'addition, s'il vous plaît.	Waiter, the bill, please.
Il n'y a pas une erreur?	Isn't there a mistake?
Le service est compris?	Is the service included?
La boisson était en sus.	The drink was extra.

What are these restaurants offering?

TARIF DES CONSOMMATIONS			
Café Express	**11.70**	Coca-Cola	**10.50**
Café Décaféiné	**11.70**	Orangina	**10.50**
Café Crème	**11.70**	Sodas	**10.50**

Plat du Jour

123 F.
Canard rôti
Petits pois

100 F.
Moules Marinières
Pommes frites

◆ **Foundation words**

la boîte	box, tin
le pot	jar
le paquet	packet
le sac	bag
la tranche	slice
la douzaine	dozen
la livre	pound
le kilo	kilo
le gramme	gram

le verre	glass
la bouteille	bottle
le litre	litre

un peu	little
ça va comme ça	that's fine
beaucoup	lot
un morceau	bit, a piece
la moitié	half

◆ **Foundation phrases**

Je voudrais un kilo de pommes.	I'd like a kilo of apples.
Quatre tranches de jambon, s'il vous plaît.	Four slices of ham, please.
Je peux avoir un morceau de ce fromage?	Can I have a piece of this cheese?
Vous avez encore des abricots?	Do you have any apricots left?
C'est tout?	Is that all?
Et avec ça?	Anything else?
Donnez-moi une boîte de carottes.	Give me a tin of carrots.

◆ **Higher words**

You might also need these words:

goûter à	to try
la spécialité	speciality
le plat	course
le supplément	extra charge

Add any other useful words here:

....

....

....

◆ **Higher phrases**

| L'addition est fausse. | The bill isn't right. |
| Vous m'avez trop fait payer. | You've overcharged me. |

CLOTHES AND SOU

◆ **Foundation words**

acheter	to buy
l'argent	money
la caisse	cash desk, till
cher	expensive
gratuit	free
trop	too, too much
bon marché	inexpensive
la liste	list
la monnaie	change
la mode	fashion
le disque	record

les vêtements	clothes
un imperméable	mac
le manteau	coat
le pardessus	overcoat
le blouson	jacket
la veste	jacket
un anorak	anorak
le chemisier	blouse
le gilet	waistcoat
le pull(over)	pullover
le tricot	jumper
la chemise	shirt
le costume	suit
la robe	dress
le T-shirt	T-shirt

| le collan |
| le slip |
| le soutie |

une pa
des ba
la bo
la ch
la cl
la p
la s

◆ **Foundation phrases**

A l'école, je porte un pantalon gris et
cravate rouge et r
A la maison, je préfère porter un je
un survête
Quand il fait froid, maman
m
Mes vêtements préférés sont me
en cuir et mon
Où est-ce qu'il fa
Je n'ai pas de

MES NO
PERSONNE

Mes Vêtem

Quand

Mes vêt

◆ **Foundation w**
la taille
la pointure
le nylon
le coton
le cuir
la laine
la couleur
court
long

◆ **Foundation phr**
Cette robe
Ces chauss
D'accord, j
Vous avez quelque
Je voudrais un im
Je voudrais

Avez-vous ce

Je vais acheter des bou

Vous avez la mé

98

◆ **Foundation words**

le parapluie	umbrella	le porte-monnaie	purse
le parfum	perfume	le portefeuille	wallet
le rouge à lèvres	lipstick	le sac	bag
la montre	watch	le jouet	toy
le mouchoir	handkerchief	la poupée	doll

◆ **Higher words**

You might also need these words: *Add any other useful words here:*

se faire rembourser	to get your money back
la fermeture éclair	zip
le polo	leisure shirt
à la mode	in fashion
démodé	out of fashion

....

....

....

◆ **Higher phrases**

Je voudrais me faire rembourser.   I'd like to have my money back.

Ce n'est plus à la mode.   That's no longer in fashion.

What are these signs about?

SEVEN STEPS TO SUCCESS

1 VOCABULARY

There are some words which look similar in both French and English but which have quite different meanings. These are called "false friends", and you need to make a careful note of such words when you meet them.

See if you can get these words right without looking back:

1 *Chips* doesn't mean "chips", but ....

2 *Une tartine* doesn't mean "a tart" but ....

3 *Une prune* doesn't mean "a prune" but ....

4 *Un plat* doesn't mean "a plate" but ....

(Answer on page 112)

2 DICTIONARY

If you are stuck, don't just write in English on the writing paper or leave a gap on the listening or reading papers: use your dictionary to come up with something in French. A sensible guess might be right, but a blank space never scores a mark.

3 LISTENING

Listen out not just for key words but also for negatives. For example, if you want to know what someone wants to drink, listen carefully, because *Je ne bois pas de ...* tells you what someone does **not** want to drink.

Numbers can be a problem and are always in the listening exam somewhere. You need to practise them a lot, but also apply common sense in the exam. Some bananas for sale for *neuf francs vingt* are unlikely to cost 29 francs. This again is where your cultural knowledge of what a French franc is worth (there are about eight to the pound) comes in. You should always write numbers or times in figures to show you have understood: *9F20* or *12.30*.

4 SPEAKING

Think carefully about the role-play and decide whether you need to use *vous* or *tu*. Which would you use in the following situations?

1 Talking to a waiter. ....

2 Talking to your penfriend or exchange partner. ....

3 Talking to a shop assistant. ....

4 Talking to your exchange partner's father. ....

(Answer on page 112)

5 **READING**
When reading a long piece, don't panic because of the length, and don't try to understand it all at once:
- Read it through two or three times, then read the questions.
- Take it section by section.
- Don't worry about every word if you can understand most of it.

6 **WRITING**
Try to write about other people, to avoid all your sentences beginning, *Je*... For example: *Mon frère et moi, nous ... Mes parents ... Ma meilleure amie ...* This means that you will have to remember the correct ending on the verb.

7 **EXAM WORK**
Look carefully at the number of marks that each question is worth: if you are asked to give two details, then make sure you do. If the question asks what somebody buys, and you hear or read *Je prends le pull rouge,* then try to give the colour as well in your answer, as the detail may be important.

◆ **Bon appetit!**
Write these items under the correct heading.

une carafe d'eau	gâteau de riz	glace au cassis
œuf mayonnaise	truite aux amandes	verre de vin rosé
bœuf bourguignon	potage du jour	pâté de saumon fumé
crème caramel	jus d'ananas	poulet à la crème

Pour commencer	Plat principal	Dessert	Boisson
....	....	....	....
....	....	....	....
....	....	....	....
....	....	....	....
....	....	....	....
....	....	....	....

(Answer on page 112)

Transport

GENERAL

◆ Foundation words

dépanner	to fix	le poids lourd	HGV
crever	to burst	le taxi	taxi
manquer	to miss	le vélo	bike
annuler	to cancel	un embouteillage	traffic jam
changer	to change	la circulation	traffic
descendre de	to get off	le piéton	pedestrian
monter dans	to get in	la sécurité	safety
partir	to leave	les transports	public transport
quitter	to leave	en commun	
prendre	to take	le péage	toll booth
contrôler	to check	l'autostop	hitch-hiking
montrer	to show		
perdre	to lose	le dépliant	leaflet
		le numéro	number
la voiture	car	la place	seat
une auto	car	prochain	next
la bicyclette	bike	rapide	fast
le camion	lorry	le retard	delay

◆ Foundation phrases

Je vais au collège à pied.	I walk to school.
J'ai un pneu crevé.	I've got a puncture.
Vous descendez à la gare.	You get off at the station.

Where would you see these signs?

Port Gare Maritime

VOIE PIÉTONNE
STRICTEMENT INTERDIT AUX 2 ROUES

SORTIE DE CAMIONS

Défense de fumer

RESTAURANT
RENSEIGNEMENTS
TELEPHONES
SALLE D'ATTENTE

TRAINS AND BUSES

◆ **Foundation words**

un (auto)bus	bus	la consigne automatique	luggage locker
un (auto)car.	coach	une entrée	entrance
le train	train	le guichet	ticket office
un express	express	un horaire	timetable
le rapide	express	les objets trouvés	lost property
le TGV	high speed train	le quai	platform
		la voie	platform, track
un arrêt	stop	la salle d'attente	waiting room
s'arrêter	to stop	la sortie	exit
la gare routière	bus station	la sortie de secours	emergency exit
le métro	underground		
la station de métro	metro station	les bagages	luggage
le chemin de fer	railway	la correspondance	connection
		la destination	destination
un aller-retour	return	assis	sitting
un aller-simple	single	debout	standing
le billet	ticket	défense de fumer	no smoking
le carnet	book of tickets	l'arrivée	arrival
la classe	class	le départ	departure
fumeur	smoking	l'eau potable	drinking water
non-fumeur	non-smoking	interdit	forbidden
le ticket	ticket	libre	free
composter	to date-stamp	occupé	occupied, engaged
le wagon-restaurant	dining car	poussez	push
le wagon-lit	sleeping car	tirez	pull
		en provenance de	from
le buffet	station buffet	les renseignements	information
la consigne	left luggage office	la réservation	reservation
		en retard	late
		le voyageur	traveller

◆ **Foundation phrases**

Le train pour Bruxelles part à quelle heure?	When does the Brussels train leave?
Le train pour Lille part dans trois minutes.	The Lille train leaves in three minutes.
Le train pour Londres part de quel quai?	Which platform does the London train leave from?
Le train de Paris a vingt minutes de retard.	The train from Paris is twenty minutes late.

Pardon, il y a un car qui va à Boulogne?	Excuse me, is there a coach which goes to Boulogne?
Cet autobus s'arrête à la gare SNCF?	Does this bus stop at the railway station?
C'est quel numéro pour aller à la plage?	Which number is it to go to the beach?
Il y a un arrêt d'autobus près d'ici?	Is there a bus stop near here?
Un aller-retour deuxième classe pour Nantes.	A second class return ticket to Nantes.
Quand voulez-vous voyager?	When do you want to travel?
Vous devez composter vos billets.	You have to date-stamp your tickets.
C'est direct?	Is it direct?
Non, il faut changer.	No, you have to change.
Cette place est occupée?	Is this seat occupied?

◆ Higher words

You might also need these words:

à l'heure	on time
prévu	scheduled
le délai	delay
le compartiment	compartment
la couchette	sleeping berth

Add any other useful words here:

....

....

....

◆ Transport puzzle

Start at the arrow and read to the centre, shading in the 7 means of transport as you go.

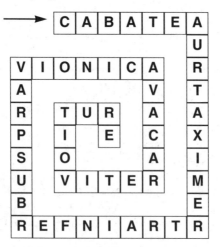

(Answer on page 112)

BOATS AND PLANES

◆ Foundation words

un aéroglisseur	hovercraft	décoller	to take off
atterrir	to land	le vol	flight
un avion	aeroplane	le supplément	surcharge
un aéroport	airport	la douane	customs

◆ Higher words

You might also need these words:

le vol de retour	return flight
l'heure de départ	departure time
le guichet d'enregistrement	check-in desk
un haut-parleur	loud speaker

Add any other useful words here:

....

....

....

....

PRIVATE TRANSPORT

◆ Foundation words

garer	to park	la station-service	petrol station
stationner	to park	le/la pompiste	petrol attendant
le stationnement	parking	l'essence	petrol
doubler	to overtake	sans plomb	lead free
faire le plein (d'essence)	to fill up	le super	4-star
vérifier	to check	le gas oil	diesel
gonfler	to inflate		
la location	to hire	s'arrêter	to stop
le moteur	engine	le vélomoteur	motorised bike
le permis de conduire	driving licence	le VTT	mountain bike
		la moto	motorbike
la ceinture de sécurité	safety belt	le véhicule	vehicle
le casque	helmet	la motocyclette	motorcycle
le pneu	tyre		
la portière	door	le pneu crevé	flat tyre
la roue	wheel	la collision	crash
le coffre	boot	en panne	broken down
le siège	seat	la déviation	diversion
les essuie-glaces	wipers	le mécanicien	mechanic
le phare	headlight	la marque	make
le pare-brise	windscreen	la vitesse	speed, gear

freiner	to brake	le code de la route	highway code
le tunnel	tunnel	d'occasion	second hand
le virage	bend	sens interdit	no entry
le passage protégé	right of way		

◆ Foundation phrases

L'autoroute est à dix minutes d'ici.	The motorway is ten minutes from here.
Faites le plein s'il vous plaît.	Fill up the tank, please.
Ma voiture est tombée en panne.	My car has broken down.
Stationnement interdit!	No parking!
Voulez-vous vérifier l'huile?	Would you check the oil?
Les essuie-glaces ne marchent pas.	The windscreen wipers won't work.

What do these signs mean?

Road signs

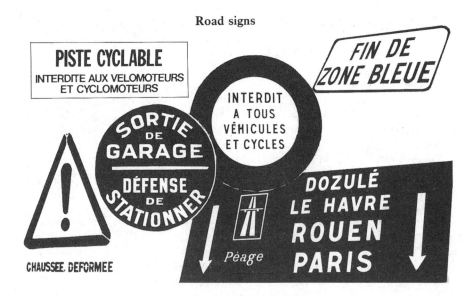

◆ **Higher words**

You might also need these words:		*Add any other useful words here:*
le volant	steering wheel	
une amende	fine	....
accélérer	to accelerate	
ralentir	to slow down	....
remorquer	to tow	
le lavage	car wash	....
		....
		....

◆ **Higher phrases**

Il est entré en collision avec un camion.	He collided with a lorry.
A quelle vitesse peut-on rouler ici?	What speed can you do here?
J'ai dû payer une amende.	I had to pay a fine.
La voiture n'a pas ralenti.	The car didn't slow down.

SEVEN STEPS TO SUCCESS

1 **VOCABULARY**
Some people try word association and other tricks to help them remember words. See if it works for you, and make some of your own up like these:

Don't *panne-ic* (panic) if your car breaks down.

Double your speed to overtake a tractor.

Consigne (consign) your cases to the left luggage office.

2 **DICTIONARY**
Use the little words in brackets in your dictionary to help you find the right word. If you want to say "The cases are in the boot" and you look up the word "boot", you might find something like (AUT) next to the word *coffre* to show you this is a word you want when talking about automobiles.

3 **LISTENING**
When answering in French, just show that you have understood the tape and are giving the right information: don't worry about the accuracy of grammar or spelling. You can often answer with a single word or short phrase: don't write full sentences unless you feel it is necessary to answer the question properly.

4 SPEAKING

Think how to adapt what you know to any situation. If you need to say "the engine won't go", but you can't think of *Le moteur ne marche pas* you might get round it with *Il y a un problème avec le moteur.* Or, if you want to say "Check the tyres please" use *regardez* if you can't think of *vérifiez*. Also, for "Is this seat taken?" use *libre* if you can't remember *occupée*.

5 READING

Check the tense of the text and the question. If you are asked to say how somebody used to get to work, and the text reads *Autrefois, je prenais la voiture pour aller à mon travail, tandis que maintenant je prends le train,* then it is the means of transport talked about in the imperfect tense that you need to give.

6 WRITING

At the beginning of sentences, try to use words like *cinq minutes après, plus tard, puis, ensuite, mais* to make your sentences read better in a paragraph.

7 EXAM WORK

You will usually have to write in French, but occasionally in English. The basic rule is: if the question is in English, answer in English, if the question is in French, answer in French. The example that is done for you will give you further help with this.

General

◆ Question words

comment	how
quand	when
qui	who
pourquoi	why
qu'est-ce que	what
combien	how much/many
quel	which
où	where

◆ Days

lundi	Monday
mardi	Tuesday
mercredi	Wednesday
jeudi	Thursday
vendredi	Friday
samedi	Saturday
dimanche	Sunday

◆ Months

janvier	January
février	February
mars	March
avril	April
mai	May
juin	June
juillet	July
août	August
septembre	September
octobre	October
novembre	November
décembre	December

◆ Seasons

le printemps	spring
l'été	summer
l'automne	autumn
l'hiver	winter

◆ Time

l'heure	time
l'heure	hour
la minute	minute
la seconde	second
demi	half
le quart	quarter
midi	midday
minuit	midnight
la semaine	week
quinze jours	fortnight
le mois	month
l'an	year

◆ Colours

blanc	white
bleu	blue
brun	brown
gris	grey
jaune	yellow
noir	black
marron	brown
orange	orange
rose	pink
rouge	red
vert	green
violet	purple
foncé	dark
clair	light

◆ Numbers 1–19

zéro	nought
un	one
deux	two
trois	three
quatre	four
cinq	five
six	six
sept	seven
huit	eight
neuf	nine
dix	ten
onze	eleven
douze	twelve
treize	thirteen
quatorze	fourteen
quinze	fifteen
seize	sixteen
dix-sept	seventeen
dix-huit	eighteen
dix-neuf	nineteen

◆ Numbers 20–1,000

vingt	twenty
vingt-et-un	twenty-one
vingt-deux	twenty-two
vingt-trois	twenty-three
vingt-quatre	twenty-four
vingt-cinq	twenty-five
vingt-six	twenty-six
vingt-sept	twenty-seven
vingt-huit	twenty-eight
vingt-neuf	twenty-nine
trente	thirty
quarante	forty
cinquante	fifty
soixante	sixty
soixante-dix	seventy
quatre-vingts	eighty
quatre-vingt-dix	ninety
cent	one hundred
mille	thousand

Answers

◆ **School crossword** page 10

1 durer, 2 cours/chimie, 3 sciences,
4 espagnol, 5 histoire, 6 travail,
7 lycée/leçon, 8 langue

◆ **Seven Steps** page 16

Vocabulary: 1 la cantine, 2 les cours,
3 L'anglais est ma matière préférée.
4 Regardez le tableau.
Dictionary: Ma matière préférée, c'est la géographie, mais je trouve le dessin très ennuyeux.

◆ **Seven Steps** pages 23–24

Vocabulary: Very useful: gagner, un médecin, l'avenir, un étudiant
Less useful: expérimenté, le boulot, raccrochez, un plombier
Dictionary: 1 coiffeuse, 2 épicière,
3 serveuse
Writing: 1 Je travaille tous les samedis dans un magasin en ville.
2 Ma sœur voudrait trouver un emploi comme hôtesse de l'air.
3 L'année dernière, pendant les vacances, j'ai cherché du travail dans une usine.

◆ **Slogans** page 28

1c, 2d, 3b, 4a

◆ **Seven Steps** page 31

Vocabulary: 1 une disquette, 2 un écran,
3 les actualités, 4 les informations

◆ **Seven Steps** page 39

Dictionary: 1 des chevaux, 2 des jumeaux,
3 des journaux, 4 des choux

◆ **Missing letters** page 43

Armoire

◆ **Seven Steps** pages 48–49

Vocabulary: 1 Généralement mon père fait le ménage après le dîner.
2 La chaîne-stéréo est à côté de la télévision.
3 Nous avons déménagé l'année dernière.
Dictionary: calme, campagne, canapé, cave, chaîne-stéréo, chaise, chambre, chauffage, cheminée, cher, congélateur, cuisine
Writing: (possible questions) 1 Où est-ce que je vais dormir?
2 Combien de chambres avez-vous?
3 Est-ce qu'il y a un jardin chez vous?
4 Tu as des animaux?

◆ **Seven Steps** page 53

Vocabulary: 1 dent, 2 main, 3 pied
Dictionary: 1 bow of a ship, 2 grief,
3 badly, 4 to crush, 5 gorge (valley)

◆ **Film titles** page 58

a) 1 The Lion King, 2 Star Wars,
3 Father of the Bride, 4 Jaws,
5 A Fistful of Dollars
b) 1D, 2A, 3E, 4C, 5B

◆ **Seven Steps** pages 60–61

Dictionary: 1 je suis sorti, 2 tu as vu, 3 il a fini, 4 nous avons fait
Writing: Le tennis, ça m'intéresse beaucoup. Mon passe-temps préféré, c'est le tennis. Je trouve le tennis passionnant.
La lecture, ça m'intéresse beaucoup. Mon passe-temps préféré, c'est la lecture. Je trouve la lecture passionnante.

◆ **Missing parts**   **page 65**
1 pension complète, 2 douches,
3 réception, 4 rez-de-chaussée,
5 dortoirs, 6 occupé

◆ **Seven Steps**   **pages 69–70**
Dictionary: 1 allumettes, 2 arrhes,
3 britanniques
Reading: 1 heures, fermeture
2 café, restaurant, alimentation
3 activités, s'amuser, loisirs, jeux

◆ **Seven Steps**   **page 74**
Vocabulary: anniversaire, accompagner,
malheureusement, correspondant,
rencontrer, agréable

◆ **Definitions**   **page 77**
1 une guerre, 2 un incendie,
3 la sécheresse, 4 une inondation

◆ **Seven Steps**   **page 81**
Dictionary: 1 Douvres, 2 Edimbourg,
3 Bretagne, 4 Bruxelles

◆ **Town grid**   **page 85**
1 cinéma, 2 office, 3 loin, 4 ville, 5 hôtel,
6 église, 7 poste.
Word: collège

◆ **Seven Steps**   **pages 86–87**
Vocabulary: 1 feminine, 2 feminine,
3 masculine
Writing: 1 où, 2 si, 3 parce que

◆ **Shop talk**   **page 88**
1D, 2E, 3A, 4C, 5B, 6F

◆ **Food wordsearch**   **page 91**
fraise, banane, salade, orange, prune,
citron, bifteck, escargot, champignon,
courgette, agneau, oignon, ananas,
chou, raisin, tomate

◆ **Seven Steps**   **page 100**
Vocabulary: 1 crisps, 2 slice of bread and
butter, 3 plum, 4 course
Speaking: 1 vous, 2 tu, 3 vous, 4 vous

◆ **Bon appetit!**   **page 101**
Pour commencer: gâteau de riz, œuf
mayonnaise, potage du jour, pâté de
saumon fumé
Plat principal: bœuf bourguignon, truite
aux amandes, poulet à la crème
Dessert: crème caramel, glace au cassis
Boisson: une carafe d'eau, jus d'ananas,
verre de vin rosé

◆ **Transport puzzle**   **page 104**
bateau, taxi, train, bus, avion, car,
voiture